De Facto Feminism:
   Essays
   Straight
   Outta
   Oakland

Judy Juanita

EquiDistance Press
Oakland, California

De Facto Feminism:
Essays Straight Outta Oakland
Copyright © Judy Juanita 2016
ISBN: 978-0-9716352-1-0

Cover design: Harper Design Group
Cover illustration: Peggy Mocine

EquiDistance Press
490 Lake Park Avenue
P.O. Box 16053
Oakland, CA 94610; or
whoknewyouknew@gmail.com

Thanks to the Rini Templeton Memorial Fund;
all interior artwork is by Rini Templeton except
for the image on page 27, which is a royalty-free
stock image. Albert H. Hart Jr. and Jamir Thomas/
John Lewis photos from family archive.

These essays evolved because my editor at The Weeklings, Jennifer Kabat, gave me a mountain of encouragement and consistently keen critique. Thanks, Jen. You made all the difference in the world. —Lady J.

This collection is dedicated to six friends whose passing in 2010 galvanized me—Alta Ray, Angelita Nalty de Vega, Vonetta McGee, Wini Madison, Katherine Kaiser, and Carolyn M. Rodgers. And to the late John Bishop. Dude, you mentored me from the great space!

Table of Contents

Introduction: The Path to Womanhood

I'm a woman. POW! Black. BAM! Outspoken.
STOMP! Don't fit in. OUCH! The lesson? Sometimes when one takes a stand one becomes a lone
wolf, a neighborhood of one, a community of one
to declare sovereignty for art, sexuality, spirituality and say-so -an individual. These essays connect
with a noble tradition of black women writers who
have spoken out, including Anna Julia Cooper and
Ida B. Wells-Barnett, Audre Lorde, Alice Walker,
Michelle Wallace, Angela Davis, bell hooks, Paula
Giddings, Michelle Alexander and Roxane Gay.
The Black Lives Matter movement is transfigur-
ing this same struggle for justice and liberation as
it champions the black female, male, youth, and
LGBT. Black lesbians spearheading this movement
are putting their bodies on the line at yet another
perilous historical moment. As I excavate my own
activism and naïvely determined black womanhood,
I explore key shifts and contradictions in black and
female empowerment. Through exploration and
unintentional trespass I've crossed boundaries of
art, sexuality, spirituality and feminism at the margins of society, where sexual-racial bullying is most
intense. Freedom fighters, word warriors and pushy
heroines have informed the public of this dilemma,
this discomfort borne of alienation, classism, sexism
and racism. I stand alongside them.

In 2013, my impossible dream came true. My first
novel *Virgin Soul* was published by Viking. I'm
old enough for Medicare but feel young at heart,

singing classic rock songs at the top of my lungs, dancing to sixties Motown in my bare feet, and cooking up this batch of essays, rigmarole, strenuousness & occasional (comic) riff.

When I was a junior in college, 1966-7, I joined the Black Panther Party (BPP). My college roommates and I were the first wave of students from San Francisco State to join the BPP. We thrust ourselves to the front of a tumultuous era and become agents for social change. After an internecine split in the BPP, our friendships survived; by 23, I had graduated and become the youngest faculty member of the nation's first Black Studies Department at San Francisco State.

After working as a teacher and journalist for a few years, I realized just how historic and remarkable the BPP, Black Arts and Black Studies movements were and began writing down important recollections of my participation and witness. These recollections led to attempts to write the stories in my head. But writing fiction and writing for newspapers are two different endeavors.

I pushed the idea of a novel to the back of my head yet never exorcised it. I got busy with the business of life, including marriage, motherhood and, as it happened, a divorce in 1974. Meanwhile, a stream of literature had begun flowing from journalists, other activists and novelists about the 60s. I read it all—including *Loose Change* by Sara Davidson about three female students in the 60s at Berkeley. I was looking for my story, which eluded me because I hadn't written it yet.

Fiction, the dream of it, began to seem hostile. I disliked contemporary fiction in the 70s and 80s, feeling it was narcissistic and a white out. I turned to nonfiction, poetry, biography and history. I published as a poet, becoming Poet-in-the-Schools in New Jersey where I had moved. I began writing plays. Eventually seventeen of my plays would make it to small stages in New York City and the Bay Area. I was acquiring skills that fed my fiction-writing, and the dream was evolving. Then one day in 1984, while I was subbing in a social studies classroom in Ridgewood, New Jersey, I opened the teacher's lesson plans. The teacher had collected newspaper and magazine articles into a plastic folder that I thumbed through, astonished. I saw my life — a whole unit of study on the Black Panther Party [BPP] in suburbia! Questions he had formulated for his students showed he was clearly left-leaning and earnest. I felt comfortable to share my BPP experiences with the students who were as astonished as I was. I'd had no contact with the BPP since moving to New Jersey twelve years earlier. Yet here it was — my past. My dream.

All the events and recollections and imagined ways to tell my story became vivid again. By then, writers, reporters and dissertation students looking for "the story" began to come, often obsequious, probing like a pediatric dentist. A body of literature specifically about the BPP grew steadily.

Another body of literature developed: the black chick lit phenomenon, heralded by Terry McMillan's *Waiting to Exhale* in 1992. It used real-life spoken language of black people, but often underplayed the complexity of black life. I wanted to use real-life spoken language and probe the complexities of the black experience.

Where was my story? Where was my truth? Who would want to read it? I could only answer these questions by writing the story, bit by bit, draft by draft. Finally I published that novel of the female foot soldier in the movement, herstory so deeply buried it took a while to excavate it.

—*Judy Juanita*

My California Childhood — a freedom childhood

Albert Haywood Hart Jr., my father and Tuskegee Airman, 332nd Fighter Group of the United States Army Air Forces, 1941-1945, deployed in Italy in 1944.

San Francisco was the sorceress with her hands out. Every time we crossed the San Francisco-Oakland Bay Bridge, we had to pay. Oakland was free; San Francisco was not. Pay me, she whispered. Pay for my wonderful dark treats, the Steinhart Aquarium with its dark wide hall lit up by tank after tank of bright gold green blue sharks dolphins whales stinger fish, cold-eyed still as-a-corpse fish that didn't blink when we tapped the thick glass with our fingernails. Pay for the Pacific Ocean and the clear sand with Playland-at-the-Beach in the background. I stood in front of gap-toothed 12-foot high, three-foot wide Laughing Sal, the wooden fat lady in perpetual residence at the beach, her freckles as big as doorknobs. She cackled at the Pacific Ocean, at the stream of frazzled parents, boisterous teenagers, noisy kids, and little colored me with braids, my skinny long legs covered with pedal pushers.[1]

[1] Judy Juanita. *Virgin Soul.* NY: Viking, 2013 (56).

If trips to San Francisco were the meringue on
the pies that my mother baked from scratch on
Sundays, Oakland was the dark gravy and the suc-
culent roast. My siblings and I chewed on it and
grew strong in a childhood centered on family,
church, playing, books and school. Three girls
and a boy, we were the second black family on a
children-filled block of identical three-bedroom
stucco houses with back doors built to catch the
bay breezes by Portuguese immigrants in the for-
ties. In the fifties, our East Oakland neighborhood
was a mosaic. We traded comics with Frankie from
Hawaii, played musical instruments with the Ojeda
sisters from Mexico, shared our grandmother's corn-
bread with the family of Mormons from Utah next
door, played hide and go seek with the Chavez kids
three doors down. We plotted outside sleepovers,
the blankets draped over poles set up in our back-
yards. Blackness was a bend in the road ahead,
nothing to think about, a sci-fi alien ship floating
on the screen of life far away. What separated us
was not race; the boys slept in one yard, the girls
another. And our front doors were unlocked.

Coming in from the cold to a breakfast of grits,
eggs, cereal, bacon and juice was worth the
newsprint-stained fingers.

My big brother Skippy (a.k.a. Skip, Skipper, even
Skippy Peanut Butter Chunky Style) ruled. I was
two years younger and a grade behind him. The
earthquakes that rumbled and once split the drive-
way half a foot wide were thrilling, but no more
threatening than the horror movies we saw for three
soda pop caps. During intermission, Skippy stood
at the concession stand and turned his eyelids inside

out and made the pupils disappear. When little kids turned and saw him, they screamed and ran, much to our delight. On Sundays we helped Skippy deliver the Oakland Tribune and the San Francisco Chronicle, my father piling us into the Ford Fairlane. I was nine. Coming in from the cold to a big breakfast of grits, eggs, cereal, bacon and juice was worth the newsprint-stained fingers.

GE, we bring good things to life, the ad on the television blared. Behind our house was the General Electric factory that didn't hire coloreds. A creek ran underneath it. Parents forbade us from the creek, warning that it carried unspeakable things from the undertaker four blocks north. But Skipper and Jimmy next door explored and found it led to the Alameda estuary and the San Francisco Bay. Jimmy's sister and I decided to go alone. We ironed our pedal pusher outfits, packed lunch and set out. The dried mud and briny water immediately dirtied our sneakers. We squatted and walked single file beneath the factory. It was disgusting but we couldn't turn back. Swatting all manner of bugs and creepy crawlies, we tromped through waist-high marsh for three hours to bring back our jar of guppies, our proof. I was better at going to the doll hospital with my mother in downtown Oakland. I loved tending my pink-cheeked porcelain dolls, braiding their yellow yarn hair and sewing their dresses and underpants.

My father, a Joe Louis look-alike,
served in WWII as a Tuskegee Airman,
332nd squadron

Friday nights we stood and saluted the flag on TV,
singing the national anthem before my dad watched
the fights. My father, a Joe Louis look-alike, had
served in the war as a Tuskegee Airman, 332nd
squadron. He never bragged and I didn't realize his
historic contribution until I got older. At the time
I only knew he loved the fights and got worked up
punching along with Sugar Ray Robinson. We loved
TV but hated choosing *I Love Lucy* on Mondays
or *Make Room for Daddy* on Tuesdays. Reading was
more important to my parents. My father, highly
intelligent, volatile, an insatiable reader of mysteries and westerns, was a "race man" and a natural
rebel. He worked several jobs, often leaving or getting fired when he wouldn't put up with demeaning
racial slurs. He developed a whole other life at the
racetrack and the poker club.

My mother, also a reader, was a sweet go-getter,
soft-spoken, deeply religious and superbly practical.
She met Dad at Langston University in Oklahoma
where he was planning to be a minister. Then he
went to war. She graduated and went to Washington, D.C., becoming part of Franklin Delano
Roosevelt's newly integrated federal civil service.
Before WWII, my father's clan had migrated on the
Santa Fe Railroad from Oklahoma to its last stop in
Berkeley to stay at an uncle's rooming house until
work was found and money saved. When my parents married she migrated to California. I was born
in Berkeley at Herrick Hospital. While working his
postal route, my father spotted our house on oblong

Eastlawn Street, a stone's throw from a large play-field and an elementary school. My mother saved for the down payment in a Mason jar. A fellow Oklahoman moved us to East Oakland on a Saturday night, a mattress falling off his truck in passage; mindlessly, my siblings and I curled up on the sofa bed in the new living room, watching *The Jackie Gleason Show* until we fell asleep.

During the Eisenhower years, Mom used to jump-start our Saturday housecleaning by saying: "What if the President of the United States came to our house tomorrow!" We'd polish and dust as if Ike himself was going to drop in. My father often worked at the cannery near our house. From early spring until late fall the refrigerator burst with peaches, apples, nectarines, plums and apricots. On rainy days, we played for hours in our parents' bed-room, trying on Dad's overcoats and my mother's high heels and rhinestone brooches, playing Nat King Cole LPs, and always, fingering the cameo of our grandfather, Mr. Hart, the rich man. When we asked about him, Dad would brush it off. But bits and pieces leaked out: *Mr. Hart had been a scout in Oklahoma for oilmen; he knew the trails because he was smitten with the Indian girls; that's where he met Momma Hart; he discovered oil; he became Oklahoma's first black oil millionaire; the white men he was dealing with went to jail; when they got out, they beat him to a pulp over the deeds and left him to die on the plains; he was never the same.* Dad would only make cryptic remarks like, "Our music room was the length of this house."

We were the first family on the block to visit Disney-land, going three summers in a row. We traveled in a trailer first to Yosemite National Park, then to

Los Angeles. At the park, we bunked in the trailer, Dad in the car in case of hungry bears. We ate fish from the river fried over the cook site. The hungry bear decided to show up while Dad was sleeping. The growling awakened us; we jumped up and rocked the trailer, waking up Dad with our screaming. The bear went away but my heart wouldn't stop pounding in the night. During the day, we played with white children from families from Idaho and Nevada while the dads fished and talked at the waterfall's edge and the mothers talked and watched us all. To get to our destination, we left Yosemite, passed Fishtown, and then drove through the dust and trucks on Route 99; once we drove parallel to a crop-duster close enough to see that it was a big bicycle with wings. When we got to the winding old Grapevine outside Los Angeles, it was night and the radio signals were fuzzy. Dad slowed to a crawl around the hairpin curves. We were told to go to sleep. I couldn't. I was petrified that our car would fall off the shoulder and crash so far down no one would want to rescue us.

A goody-goody, I was in no way immune to malicious mischief. My friends and I fooled around on the phone, calling boys we had crushes on and hanging up, dialing numbers at random and asking, "Is your refrigerator running?" To the few who replied, we'd say, "You better go catch it." My worst phone mischief took place at the height of the Mickey Mouse Club mania. Every TV-watching kid in the country dreamed of becoming a Mouseketeer. Z___ was a precocious student a grade under me. Her parents fancied her a child prodigy and showered her with lessons—piano, violin, viola, voice, tap, ballet. We thought she was nothing but a big baby, but she performed at school assemblies as if she was about to be discovered any minute. One afternoon after fooling around on the phone, we concocted a scheme. After practicing our fake voices a bit, we dialed Z__'s number. She answered and we went into our act. "This is a representative of Walt Disney. We've received notices of your outstanding talent and want you to come to Hollywood and audition for the Mickey Mouse Club."

She fell hook, line and sinker for it. We led her on and on with increasingly fabulous offers of money, contracts and free hotel stays on Sunset Strip. We could hardly keep from laughing out loud. Finally we ran out of details and got annoyed that she couldn't see through it all. We broke it to her ungently. Flustered, she queried us. "Are you sure you're not from Disney?" When we identified ourselves she cried.

Somewhere along the way my father's gambling became compulsive and finances strained. Household items, bikes, radios would disappear and show up weeks or months later. When the Big Bopper and Richie Valens died in a plane crash, my best friend and I hurried home to watch *American Bandstand*. In the living room, where the TV console had reigned, was an empty space. Dad had hocked the TV. At another point we placed cardboard in our shoes when they wore out too fast. During this period I noticed that, in church, some people got more respect than others. It seemed to be tied to money, late-model Cadillacs, and nice clothes and furs, the kind with the dead raccoon faces flipped over the shoulder. Others — the ones with an endless line of stairstep children and meager resources, seemed to be objects of pity. Although Skip and

I were touted as the smartest in the bunch, I was deeply ashamed of being pitiable. I couldn't begin to understand why my mother insisted I pray at the altar in my cardboard shoes. I tried to kneel to keep my soles flat on the floor but it was impossible. My cheeks burned so hard I thought they would burst. My feeling for church changed permanently.

Until I left home, I attended church every Sunday inexorably following the preacher's humming and call-and-response, the elaborate twisting of biblical stories and characters into present day parables. But as adolescence approached I preferred traveling with the gospel choir. An elaborate interfaith visitation of exchange choirs united black churches in Oakland, Berkeley, Richmond, and Seaside near Monterey, Vallejo and Pittsburg. I gorged on the different gospel singers with utterly unique, surging voices, vocal gyrations and styles, the ubiquitous down home cuisine. I heard Ruthie, Anita and Pat Pointer sing at their father's church in West Oakland long before they became the Pointer Sisters. I knew of Sylvester Stewart from his father's Vallejo pastorate before he became disc jockey and then rock star Sly Stone.

Sixth grade presented another demarcation. I represented the school in the citywide spelling bee and found, to my dismay, that a clique of girls had cheered on one of its own who was terminally ill with leukemia. When the girls taunted and ostracized me for winning I threw up at school, breaking a perfect attendance record. That alerted my mother. When I broke down and told her why I was miserable, she told me that even if everybody else was doing wrong, I should be the one to follow conscience. I didn't understand what conscience had to do with being the best speller but the admonition was one she and my father repeated often: *don't follow the crowd*. I buried myself in books, carried a book everywhere, read under the covers with a flashlight after bedtime, all the while counting the days to the end of sixth grade.

I was unaware that I was about to shed my neighborhood friends. My mother wisely encouraged me to make black girlfriends at church although I wondered why churches were segregated if God was above all. The girls on my block found new white friends; I became close to the three other black girls in college prep. We played instruments—I played string bass—and began traveling to orchestra and band competitions throughout the region. Our cheap thrill was to cut class on Fridays and ride the bus to the main library in downtown Oakland where we sneaked potato chips and sweets and listened to symphonic music.

I loved music and dancing. I practiced dancing with girlfriends and the doorknob to R&B and top 40s. At my first nighttime dance, an older boy, James, asked me to dance. Two grades ahead of me, he already had shaving bumps. It was rumored he wanted to be a priest. Why priest and not minister I couldn't think through. I was ecstatic to be on the dance floor. We were Texas-hopping to the music when he stopped point blank.

"Loosen your grip," he said.

I dropped his hand and he said, "You've been dancing with the doorknob, haven't you?"

I nodded, he laughed and we continued, my wrist limp. I mastered all the dances—cha-cha, hully gully, slop, chicken, funky chicken, strand, Slauson shuffle, the Boston, jerk, pony and twist, everything except my sister's forte, the mashed potatoes. The annual R & B talent show put on by the black Greek fraternities was called The Jabberwock. It was an occasion for dressing up, listening to three hours of good, mediocre and astonishing local talent. When the locally famous duo Don and Juan sang their hit "What's Your Name?" the audience went crazy. Besides the requisite light skin and curly hair, they had good voices. During the middle of their number, either Don or Juan opened his mouth wide to hit a note and a set of false teeth popped out. He grabbed for them but they landed in the front rows. Goners. Don and Juan ran offstage to loud laughter. Ridicule and disdain threaded the needle of adolescence.

Slowly I became aware of the high status of light skin and nonkinky hair, of intraracism though I didn't call it such fancy names. My ear pressed to his bedroom door, I gleaned from my brother and his buddies the rules of color caste. I understood that being smart had absolutely no sexual importance. They rated girls foxy on the basis of skin color, big legs, curvy bottoms and cute faces, long or semi-straight hair. About one particularly shapely, light skinned girl with pronounced African features and thick glasses, they constantly conjured up sex with a paper bag over her head.

In a world that I had yet to understand in a larger historical context, age, family and church hemmed me in. In high school, a girlfriend and I often ran into a woman that we called the white-faced lady in downtown Oakland. A brown skinned woman, in her thirties, she wore white makeup smeared over her face, hands, and legs, white or pastel clothes, white stockings and shoes. It seemed like she always came right up behind us; we'd turn and scream at the sight. We heard two explanations for her behavior: one, she was mentally unbalanced; and two, she had married a fellow white UC student who left her and never got over him.

By tenth grade, I had to cart my string bass home a considerable distance. Junior high had been around the corner. With 1,500 fellow sophomores, Castlemont High was challenging. Another bass player, Phil Escovedo, hardly seemed to attend school and played a different way anyhow. He told me he was playing with his cousins in nightclubs for $10 and suggested I could too. I knew my mother better than to ask. I stopped playing bass after tenth grade and followed my brother, the sports editor, onto the school paper. I loved writing and hanging out with that crowd. The newsroom became my home, the advisor, Roland Christensen, like an uncle. With his mentoring, I became a reporter. By graduation, he nominated me for Outstanding Journalism Student. I was to graduate with honors. But just shy of seventeen I was still prankish. Mr. Christensen had bought a huge cake for the department, which by Friday afternoon was still half-eaten. Not wanting bugs to eat the cake over the weekend, I started handing out generous squares to friends who were picking up their prom pictures. When Mr. Christiansen found out, he hit the roof, threatening to prevent me from graduating onstage, let alone receiving the award. I spent a weekend in agony, wondering how to tell my parents. By Monday, his temper had cooled and the threat became a last lecture. I graduated (with 600 others) and got the award. A kindly church elder wrote on my graduation card: "You've crossed the river. Ahead is the ocean."

Ahead were Oakland City College (now Merritt), militants, marijuana, sexual freedom and assassinations. Death I hardly knew yet—Sam Cooke shot outside a cheap motel, my best friend and I rushing home from school to mourn Buddy Holly and Ritchie Valens on "American Bandstand"—no one close. The white families left the block for the suburbs. My sister, nine years younger, grew up on the same block with mostly black families. Skyline, the hill high school, opened my senior year and abruptly changed the racial mix of all the city's high schools, pulling from the well-off hill neighborhoods. At age sixteen years and eleven months, childhood was over. *Ovah.* The freedoms my parents had left Oklahoma for and fought for during WWII became the very rights I would battle for as a campus militant.

I would not realize how fully, peculiarly and tightly loved I was until I left California—the state and the state of mind.

San Pablo Avenue

Is it still the longest street in northern California? We drive down this old wide street,
Oakland to Berkeley to Richmond, my father,
his walker and I, out and about. It's a nice day,
a good day. We pass his haunts: key club, the
Hotel California where colored couldn't play,
the Social Club where they did, the integrated
Oaks Club. As he passes his gambling joints, a
faint smile crosses his face. I wonder: is Dad
ready to go?

Does he see what I see? Does he see what
the pawnshop gobbled like a wolf hungry and
salivating outside our door? Bicycles, the huge
console television, plastic transistor radios,
the iron. Does he see me heating the heavy
cast iron on the stove and scorching my white
blouse every time? The wolf wanted everything
we could give it, just everything, even a house
gambled away in all night poker.

We pull up to the temple in a town beyond
San Pablo. Dad chants with me at home. I
want him to chant with me here. Two young
men politely try to help my father when he
lifts a weak leg out. As they tug him out of
the car, all at once he decides he's not going.
We've driven all this way, past every sordid
boarded-up, closed-down, gone-to-seed, burnt-
to-the-ground landmark of his gambling years.
I want this redemption for him but he'll have
none of it. His jaw sets and he mutters *don't
push your religion down my throat.*

I get bubbling boiling cauldron-in-my-chest mad.
I go inside and chant while he sits in the car
and listens to jazz. I want redemption all right.
I want everything back. Just everything. I want
the bicycles, the TV, the radios, the iron, the
white blouses, and all the moments, each and
every one, before the wolf began to blow the
bricks to the ground.

It takes awhile, but after I chant I feel better.
We drive back down San Pablo Avenue. He
looks around with the exact same expression,
the same faint smile. We pass Golden Gate
Fields, the big clock next to the freeway (post
time: 1pm). I slow down as we pass the grand-
stand. It demands that. It is empty and quiet. As
we pass I can't help but hear the announcer's
nasal staccato, the horses' hooves pounding the
sod, the crowds jumping out of their seats, the
sigh of the losers, the brash laugh, all of a kind,
from the winners. I see Dad, his hair black and
curly and trimmed just so, his mustache black
and full. I smell his chewed-up cigar, watch him
handicap the daily double and fold the racing
form under his arm. As clear as the trumpet's
call to the post, I hear his *hey buddy, whatcha
know good.*

White Out

American society was one big happy family in the 1950s. A melting pot, a Jell-O & white bread land of perfection and gleaming surfaces. Not for a minute. The truth was that America was one big white out.

Growing up in the 50s, my siblings and I had to choose Make Room for Daddy or I Love Lucy for school night television. On Sunday nights, the whole family watched The Ed Sullivan Show on our one set, the high point being when a performer of our race came on. (We didn't use the word black in self-description then.)

The famous colored pop artists—Sammy Davis Jr., Johnny Mathis, Leslie Uggams, Dionne Warwick, and Nat King Cole—were so extraordinarily talented they seemed to glow. And yet they looked, to my adolescent eyes, like gifted pets of benevolent white mentors (Frank Sinatra, Mitch Miller, and Burt Bacharach), a status that befit the show's colorful menagerie of chimps, flamenco dancers and sensations like Elvis Presley. Colored performers and musicians who seemed of independent mind — Harry Belafonte, Richie Havens, and Odetta — had careers in folk or bluegrass further from the mainstream.

The poet Amiri Baraka would say later the only good thing about television back then was that colored people weren't on it. There was a loss of dignity when black people entered the arena of television as maids, mammies, butlers, shoeshine boys, and had to do what white and white-minded directors and producers wanted them to do. Anyway, we weren't for the most part on TV, except for Beulah and a token on Star Trek. We were nowhere in advertising.

The 50s meant crew cuts, skinny ties, matching suits, Teen Angel, the Beachboys, the top 40 playlist, 45 rpm records, spinning the songs. But in the parallel America, Rhythm & Blues (R & B) artists were busy providing the gritty backdrop to the violence and oppression of the American dream. Rioters, marchers, protestors and regular folk followed a different drummer, doing as a popular 1964 song advised: getting "right down to the real nitty gritty." The breathlessness of the countdown to the top 15 hits on "The Lucky Strike Hit Parade" matched the breathlessness of state-sanctioned executions, which occurred with the same exciting regularity.

Amiri Baraka said the only good thing about TV was that colored people weren't on it

1963 was a banner year for the black race. Things were heating up in the streets. That April, Martin

Luther King wrote "Letter from Birmingham Jail" to white clergymen who wanted racial segregation addressed exclusively in courts, not the streets. The next month, Bull Connor set fire hoses and attack dogs on the marchers in Birmingham. August saw The March on Washington, timed to commemorate the Emancipation Proclamation's 100th anniversary— a great peak for the civil rights movement.

The miracle of television was a lucky strike for the civil rights movement. The abolitionist movement 100 years earlier had gained traction once the world, i.e. London society, understood the horror and treachery of slavery from ex-slaves like Frederick Douglass speaking abroad or from ex-slave narratives. And similarly the civil rights movement gained universal spotlight once viewers saw the hosing, brutality, flaming buses and overturned normalcy of a South under siege from arch segregationists and protestors.

The England/America exchange of influence went back and forth. At a Beatles concert in Plymouth, Great Britain, in November 1963, police used high-pressure hoses on screaming fans, a show of authority that matched the hosing of demonstrators in Birmingham six months earlier.

This hip-click to the off beat was the way black kids danced

Meanwhile, there I was, a black girl in East Oakland, playing string bass in my junior and senior high school orchestras. As we toured school festivals throughout northern California, my fellow bassist, a member of the Escovedo musical family, tried to lure me into nightclubs for $10 a night gigs.

I knew better than to mention that to my strict Christian mother. But I loved music and craved it, especially Bo Diddley, Motown, and salsa. I'd dance in front of my mirror for six hours at a clip.

Diddley fused a 3-2 clave with rhythm and blues, and rock and roll. A Bo Diddley beat was clave-based, clave being the name of the patterns played on two hardwood sticks in Afro-Cuban music ensembles. This syncopated accent on the "off beat" was perfect for the click-and-slip of my pelvis as I bopped around my bedroom dance floor in my early teens. I thought I had invented a new dance until I started partying and found that this hip-click to the off beat was the way black kids danced in the Bay Area. Thank goodness for osmosis.

In 1963 Sly Stone was a hip young DJ who hadn't yet changed his birth name of Sylvester Stewart. He was fresh out of Vallejo and the CME/AME church gospel choir circuit I attended as a youth. He was firing up listeners in the San Francisco Bay Area on KSOL which he nicknamed K-SOUL. I had a painful crush on him.

My Oakland, pre 1964, was house parties, spiked punch, segregated radio and five-channel TV, ser-vicemen getting off the ships at the Port of Oakland looking for a good time. My Oakland, post 1964, was sets (nobody said house party, they said, "Are you going to the set on Snake Rd.?"), marijuana, stoned white college boys in khakis, hippies in VW buses covered in psychedelic colors, Make Love Not War signs and longer hair on everybody. First came the swivel hipped Elvis, then Beatlemania, then the floodgates opened.

When I first heard the Beatles, I got a pure musical thrill. When I bumped into a black girl on the steps at college listening to "I Want to Hold Your Hand" on her plastic transistor radio, her passion got my attention, all the more strange because she was black. Crushing on the Beatles, she held onto a .45 of the song like it was a rare gem.

Being a black urban teen, I was into Motown, the Temptations, James Brown, Chuck Berry, the Supremes and the Moonglows. I didn't crush on the Beatles like I did with Sly, Eddie Kendricks and David Ruffin. But that's the good thing about it.

Of course, I didn't know what was happening technically, that on "Please Please Please" and "I Want to Hold Your Hand," the Beatles used a double back beat, i.e. an off beat played as a one quarter note. But I knew something even better—I could dance to it. The Beatles, a convergence of R&B and pop, brought a great swinging movement from blond to dark, from privileged surfer children in the suburbs to the darkness of Liverpool's working class, an amalgam that curiously celebrated its R&B roots.

When these white females let it rip, they freed up black women from whoredom, from bearing the brunt and hard edge of the white man's sexuality

Neither white nor black parents could control what happened after The Pill. By the time I watched the Beatles on Ed Sullivan in 1964 in my parents' living room I had started college and knew a lot more about sex than I let on to my mother and father. All the prepubescent and adolescent white girls having orgasmic and orgiastic responses in public released a long suppressed sexuality from its Victorian,

Southern, and Puritan constraints. As these women let it rip in that prolonged moment of free public expression, they freed up black women from whoredom, from bearing the brunt and hard edge of the white man's sexuality. We were no longer the only culturally-sanctioned objects of naughty or forbidden sex, of plantation promiscuity. Stripping, nudity, free sex, skinny dipping, open marriage, group sex— sexuality came out of the closet and into the open.

Giddy with our post-high school hipness, my best friend and I regularly drove to San Francisco and hopped the cable car up to a nightclub called Copacabana West where we danced with abandon all night. I didn't know about the connection to my black roots. Or that the United States embargo against Cuba cut off Americans from overt knowledge of the Cuban influence on music, especially R & B. I just loved being able to mambo, rumba, and cha-cha with a different partner for every spin on the floor. I loved the 20 and 30 minute sets. Before the age of 18, we had been dying to get into Finnochio's, the all-male drag nightclub in North Beach that was like forbidden fruit. Finally we got past the velvet rope. Ugh! The make-up looked caked, wigs ratty, clothing dirty and drag too uncool to be enjoyable, let alone believable. One more disassembling of the American sociocultural foundation underneath me.

Just as Finnochio's female impersonators would give way decades later to the Perpetual Sisters of Indulgence, and just as the gay pride, sexual freedom and gender equality movements toughened up, American media and TV's white out would be toppled by musical, cultural and social protest.

Some look at the Beatles and say they appropriated black R&B, that they exploited it. But they acknowledged it as elemental and, by doing so, opened the door for Ike and Tina Turner, James Brown and a host of performers—once colored, now black—to share some of the rewards. Touring abroad helped many acts from the chitlin circuit beat the fabled seven year lifespan of American pop music acts and extend their showbiz longevity abroad. (Getting their health to hold out and resisting drug abuse would prove as daunting a task as overcoming segregation.)

White wasn't completely out, but black was seeping in.

It only took Dick Clark until 1983 during "Motown 25: Today, Yesterday and Forever" to publically admit what was really going down in American music in the 50s and 60s:

> As much as any other force in this industry, Motown caused a revolution in music. It was a quiet revolution but the ripple effect is still being felt all over the world. What Motown did was change our perception about black music and the people who made it. Now, until Motown came charging out of Detroit, about the only thing— genuinely black thing about mainstream music—was the vinyl from which the records were pressed....in the 50s and 60s, it was a common practice for white artists to take a song from a black performer and make their own version and come out with a big hit...those records

were called cover records....Everybody
from Elvis to an artist who later was
to record for Motown, Pat Boone, did
it. Until Motown, most of American
record buyers didn't go looking for black
records since they had hardly ever heard
the real thing. By the end of 1964, most
of the teenagers were dancing in the
streets and they wanted Martha and
the Vandellas singing to it....Kids of all
colors started hitting the record stores.
For Motown acts alone, they had 42 hits
from which to choose. That also created
a little confusion. There were certain
areas that wouldn't stock an album with
a black face on the cover.

With the Beatles and the British invasion, black
music and rock joined for a new backdrop to the
morality play called American society. White wasn't
completely out, but black was seeping in. The Beatles
brought black music to the foreground — on stage,
front and center.

Like a slap in the smug mug of white America,
the Brits acknowledged black roots. They showed
how white America had unapologetically ripped
off black people for centuries, never giving them
credit for inventing the new American art forms
of jazz, gospel, blues and R&B. America never had
been held accountable to blacks, morally, fiscally or
legally. It's not too much to say the Beatles helped
bridge the wide gulf between colored and white
America.

Five Comrades in The Black Panther Party, 1967-1970

 Bobby Seale and Huey Newton came to SF State in the spring of '67 to recruit at the same time Clorox, Kaiser and IBM came. The two men stood side by side, gave their spiel, their sign up sheets laid out in the back of the room. My roommates and I wore our hair natural and favored pea coats, ponchos and boots. But I hesitated when they signed to join the BPP, remembering my civil servant mother's warning about signing my name to radical causes.

While some came to call it the Summer of Love, for those of us in the belly of the beast-urban America, it was another long, hot summer. In August I joined. We five young women became the first wave of students from San Francisco State to join the Black Panther Party. We were referred to as sisters with skills. Evelyn handled finances, Janice became Bobby Seale's scheduler, Betty managed the BPP office, and Jo Ann corralled the troops. I worked on the BPP Intercommunal Newspaper with Eldridge and Kathleen Cleaver.

Some of the first issues of the paper were laid out at The Black House. It's no coincidence that that stately Victorian on Broderick St. was a prime gathering spot for poetry readings, jazz sets and political talks. Poets, dancers, musicians, students, party people and the lumpen mixed for a time at this home of Eldridge Cleaver and poet-playwright

Marvin X. The Black House unity didn't last; the cultural nationalists, who advocated a blacks-only cultural milieu, and the militant Panthers, who welcomed alliances with radical whites, split.

The Panthers were creating a new language, what Jean-Paul Sartre calls superlanguage. Sartre calls it language distortion, a means by which the colonized deconstruct their oppression and reorder existence. Police became pigs; a deadly police raid became a reign of terror. We made the language, as Sartre identifies it, revolutionary and incantatory: Off the pigs. Power to the people. All power to the people. Free Huey.

Sartre calls it language distortion, a means by which the colonized deconstruct their oppression and reorder existence.

Our gang of five affected policy and high-level decisions by virtue of our intense participation, outspokenness, our spacious Potomac St. flat which became a safe house, our connections to our families and communities in Oakland, Hunters' Point, the Sunset and Fillmore districts, and Iowa (shout out to Janice) where we grew up. Our parents and relatives provided money, housing, books, cars, meeting places, food and clothing to the party, as documented by the FBI.

We also formed liaisons and romantic relationships with brothers in the party. From the upper echelon to the lumpen proletariat, we lived, slept, ate and cooked with the BPP, running up and down the state and the country, all of which was a natural development that resulted in many discussions on Potomac St. about the differences (and similarities) between brothers from the street and brothers on campus. We were the initial link between the campus and the party. Three of us married "brothers in the struggle" who also happened to be educated brothers. This is significant because our connections and intimacy (which some labeled promiscuity) connected brothers from the party with brothers from SF State. The BSU brothers like to talk about supplying the BPP with guns and money, but this bridge called my back supplied the people's army with equal and greater provision.

When Huey was arrested and jailed in the shootout in November 1967, the paper overnight became an international organ, and the BPP an international sensation. To the world the party surfaced as the radical arm of the civil rights movement. At that point, my work stepped up with the paper. Donations poured into the office for the Free Huey movement. Police and FBI surveillance intensified. Six months later, the killing of Bobby Hutton and the shooting/jailing of Eldridge led to a meeting outside in Mosswood Park in Oakland, across the street from Kaiser Permanente Hospital. We met in the park because we didn't want the FBI to hear the tape from Huey. On it, he reorganized the party, and to my surprise, appointed me editor-in-chief during Eldridge's jail stay.

My friends and I dropped out of college and worked in the BPP full time.

This changed all the dynamics. School became irrelevant. SF State had been indifferent and even hostile to Negro students for so long that the strongest sense of belonging had come from black sororities and fraternities. However, after going down South and participating in the Freedom Rides in the summer of 1966, a multiracial contingent of students returned to radicalize the campus. Those students developed the Tutorial Program at SF State into a community-based web of free after school tutoring centers in the Mission, Fillmore and Potrero Hill. This campus program was a first concrete radicalization for many. My roommates and I tutored and ran several of the centers.

Many idealistic students in the sixties dropped out and some devoted lives to the movement; by the time they returned to campus, many had changed their class affiliation. My friends and I dropped out and worked in the BPP full time. We eventually returned to campus too, armed, not only with actual weapons, but with a new consciousness about education, service, the poor, the police and the military, oppression, and civil and human rights. Our experience in the party helped us envision a viability in revitalizing and connecting to our community versus fleeing into the mainstream, corporate America or the professions as a distanced, glancing downward teacher or social worker. No matter our background, and all five of us came from two-parent, middle-class families, we became aware of the class contradictions in the American dream.

I saw Bobby Seale recently and had to remind him who I was by recalling the roommates. He said, quite sincerely, "Which one was my girlfriend?" I wasn't insulted. After all, he was looking back 40 years, and we were far more than girlfriends.

Black Womanhood #1[1]

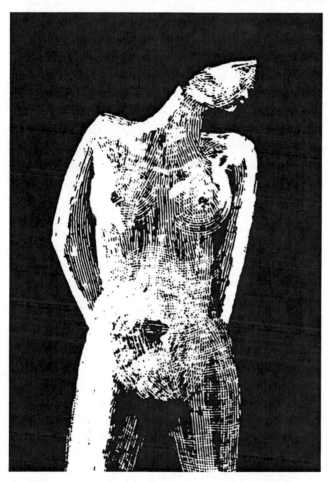

At this stage in the black revolution, the relationships between black men and black women are taking on new and crucial meanings. We need to constantly analyze and evaluate our position and

---

[1] An earlier version of this essay first appeared in the BPP Intercommunal News Service, spring 1967.

direction, in relation not only to each other, to ourselves, to the black community, and to our enemy. With the black revolution being no more than the fusing of separate frustrations, desires, convictions and strengths toward a common liberation, the black man and his woman cease to be simply a couple, two lovers, a man and his mistress, a pairing of looks or a sparring match, but a fusing, a deepening of two black minds, souls and bodies passionately involved not only in each other in "the movement," in the black community, in the Third World, in black liberation, in life itself.

One significant change taking place and at a remarkable speed is the move of the black bourgeois-oriented female into black womanhood. To understand the full implications of this move is to understand the forces stimulating it, the background and orientation of the bourgeoisie and the changes to which the move leads.

The first and foremost stimulus is and will be the black man. Women are attracted to men and black men are, in this moment, the only men on the scene. Women gravitate toward life, and the black man holds within the strength and the fiery passion of his struggle, his own life, the life of his people and his posterity. His total commitment to his life is an invitation to the black woman to join with him in the pursuit of a life together, removing the shackles of White Racist America (WRA) and establishing a solid foundation of blackness from which to build.

The second formidable stimulus is WRA. As it becomes increasingly apparent that whitey means business when he tells, in his many ways, "nigguhs ain't shit," the repetition of history becomes an overt and pressing danger. Concentration camps are no longer relegated to history. Check out John A. Williams' chilling King Alfred Plan.[2] And with their increasing possibility comes the black woman's intuition that her strength is needed as never before... her strength, not her will, her leadership, her domination, but her strength. And she comes, from all levels of Negro life, bringing with her the heritage of her mother, 400 years of bearing the burden of two families (the white man's and her own), discarding the stench of his foul body, his foul morality, his foul domesticity and his foul, disillusioning, glorified mainstream. In its place she brings her belief in the black man, her own sensuality and her strong back. She comes to the black man from this to this.

The actual move comes at the end of a process of disintegration of those values of WRA, which the black bourgeoisie strives hardest to emulate. The most dominant value which bourgies embrace is materialism and/or the great American dream. Wrapped inextricably with this is American (im)morality and individualism or alienation.

Toward men this materialism is ingrained in the attitude of bourgeois women, sexually, socially and economically. The bourgeois female, i.e., young, whorish, working, extremely well-dressed (on $350 a month) and as near in simulated looks and makeup, stance and blandness as possible to the Glamour-Mademoiselle-Vogue image (which changes with age to Ebony-Ladies Home Journal-McCall's image), uses and emasculates her man as a

---

[2] John A. Williams. *The Man Who Cried I Am.* Boston: Little Brown, 1967.

social coat-hanger, a bill-payer, a dude, a vehicle to further her own confused self-image…a nigger.

The emasculation concept is not just thrown in as an aside on my part. The Negro woman's disrespect for and hatred of her man is an integral part of her functioning. She comes from a home in which the man is nothing more than an accessory to her mother, and as often as not, grandmother, aunt and other dominant matriarchal figures. A house in which the male can't function unless he's drunk, it's the first of the month, or he's physically asserting himself, either by yelling, beating or fucking.

Good grief. Am I sounding like Daniel Moynihan? I learned my oppressor's language well. Could we be saying the same thing about matriarchy in the black community? Am I trying to reverse his theory? In *Black Orpheus*, Sartre says, "Having been dispersed to the four corners of the earth by the slave trade, black men (and women) have no common language; in order to incite the oppressed to unite, they must necessarily rely on the oppressor's language ….since the oppressor is present in the very language they speak, they will speak this language in order to destroy it."[3]

The bourgie girl uses her sexuality as a convenience. His penis is of no less importance to her than a kitchen appliance i.e. it is used. He doesn't make love to her; he fucks. He moves in and out, just as she wishes. They masturbate mutually.

Their relationship on the emotional level reflects its own morality. There is no trust, no faith, no

---

[3] Jean-Paul Sartre and John MacCombie. Black Orpheus, The Massachusetts Review, Vol. 6, No. 1 (Autumn, 1964—Winter, 1965).

companionship, no basis for growth and development. They meet, probably at a gig, and embrace
each other as two ships passing in the middle of
the night. We see the bourgies coming together
and each insecure in their "whiteness move further
apart from themselves. We see them constantly
one-upping one another. Both out dress each other.
Both have the latest cars. Both read Playboy. Both
try their hardest to embrace the American dream.
They quit each other and sail frantically towards
another ship. As they get older, we see the same
"out-doing" the other one taking place, their dual
achievements reinforcing their separateness, alienat-
ing their entities. Each has a jar, a car, an education,
a psychiatrist, a bed, each gets a divorce and each
has a child.

It is from this perpetual vacuum that bourgeois
chicks proceed to their black womanhood. Her
former role is not even reversed but abolished. There
is no time for what went on before to continue —
no time at all. WRA is a time bomb. And black
women reciprocate by developing full blown a womanhood in which her man and thus commitment
becomes the essence of her life. He moves from the
periphery to the center. He becomes the center.

Politically, economically, socially and sexually, a
new ethic is molded, constantly adapting itself to
the needs of blackness.

She stops pressing her hair to show both her man
and Charlie that she is ready to accept her womanhood and all the responsibilities and privileges
it entails. She becomes involved in her community
with the end in mind of laying the foundation for
the man's destruction. It is indicative of the times

to see formerly ultra-bourgies refocus and reorient their lives. They move back from the middle-class suburbs and outer limits of the cities into the ghetto and the heart of black urbania.

Economically, she reorients her status-conscious mind and gears her desires to those concomitant with black liberation. If need be, she works from 8 to 5 and brings home the money in refutation of the American rule that the man in the family brings home the money, this standard existing precisely because, in WRA, money is the equivalent or substitute for manhood.

Socially, the Negro man becomes extinct. Social barriers and distinctions disappear, replaced by a communal unity. Socially, women, who hold on hardest to status distinctions, begin to recognize there are no differentiations between black people. To WRA we are all "niggers" and we have to function in view of this label. The family assumes more than a dinner table, church-pew role, but becomes a base for activity. The man-woman relationship is a renewal-fulfillment-strengthening ongoing one in which the man ceases to be the breadwinner but becomes the element around which the woman stabilizes, catalyzes, anchors and from which children evolve, not happen.

Sex becomes not a necessary convenience but a vital, pleasurable, functional part of the whole. The sexual relationship becomes a source of strength, pleasure, renewal, mutual reinforcement, and thus enhances and redirects the total relationship, instead of determining and being the relationship. Sartre says that it is not simply "the black man's self-portrayal that seems poetic to (him), it is also his personal way of utilizing the means of expression at his disposal….in him the light of white words is refracted, polarized and altered….the black man must therefore find death in white culture in order to be reborn with a black soul, like the Platonic philosopher whose body embraces death in order to be reborn in truth….it is the dialectical law of successive transformations which leads the Negro to coincidence with himself in negritude."

Sartre wrote this in 1948 about Francophone black poets. But we are part of the same African diaspora. In terms of our survival, right now, the black man needs a woman as a base, an anchor, a refuge, a shelter, a place of peace, an institution of strength. The black woman has her own turbulent and dialectical process of self-transforming. I know because I'm living it every day.

Tough Luck

I came back to poetry when I was out on a limb.

I had walked off a daily reporting gig in northern New Jersey in an idealistic huff. Landing up shit's creek, I clutched my eight-year old son and paddled through a nasty divorce. A clump of poems lay stuffed in a dresser drawer. One afternoon, while reading the newspaper I had fled, I discovered a local poetry group called The Bergen Poets. On impulse I found it met that night, grabbed some poems and practically skipped to the house of a woman, Dorothy, I would come to know and love.

As I approached her picture widow, the sight of a roomful of white people stunned me. *What am I doing?* My feet kept moving. *I'm black.* I had forgotten that. They motioned me in, a sprinkling of poets— middle-aged, young, warm, chatty, open—listening to each other…and to me. When we broke for coffee, one young man, John, who I would also grow to love, said my work was "an embarrassment of riches" and showed me how to edit right there on the spot. His suggestions were excellent. Week after week, I brought work. The new kid on the block reworked very little old work; new poems appeared. I felt like a baby letting loose a deafening cry. Newly single, newly named, in a strange new town (Ridgewood, N.J.) that looked like a toy town far from marital hell, I started reading with my new friends at venues like The Beaten Path in Hoboken and getting published in journals like *Croton Review* and *Painted Bride Quarterly*.

momma love you yepper do

momma love you yepper do big ole baby boy
love to slap her red red bag of mad against
your suedesoft baby buttock

momma love you never likes to swim the
Sea of Tears
find that ragged lobster claw snapcrack
shell of hate
that swacks your baby bootie end to end your
baby smile
to sad

momma love you little poopie even pooping
in your pants
and playing till your poops hang low as fishies
in a net

momma love you all the whacking slapping
hitting spitting

in your sleep momma with her daddyhands
her daddystrength
her daddymight makes right

momma love you even when you sang a
sweetie peetie kicked
and whipped for stealing gum   in tubs
you sang and whistled
like a chirp in water hot to etch your whip-
ping twice into the nerve

momma love you yepper do watching for your
footsteps
through the door fishing in yim smokesoaked
redrimmed eyes

oh you smile those eyes at what they saw big
ole baby boy
taking all the touching tough inside those
brown big eyes

momma love you yepper do more for
all the less
the switch the swack the slapcheek shriek
the speedy harsh caress

momma love you yepper do how were you
to know
momma love you yepper do love you yepper do

Painted Bride Quarterly, 1983

I was published and broke, smart and broke, single-
parenting and broke. I had gotten to the intersection
where Life St. meets Riding on Fumes. I needed
a job before an 18-wheeler barreled through and
knocked baby and me off my feet.

At the Cianci St. bar

for every some one
any apt body her
sweet warm kisses
at the Cianci St. bar

float on the tip her aura
tonight free rash and tired
but not too
for tonight her

kisses are sweet rapt
rosé dried and warmed
by the great
falls flow

a bus ride away from
her shanty tear town
aprilshowered
with celibacy

this night her kisses
warm and winelip sweet
in early eve her
she at the bar

holds the eve
in the tip of
her budded
beer

Through contemplating my navel, I won an artist fellowship and got appointed Poet-in-the-Schools from the New Jersey State Council on the Arts, where I met my next mentors, the poets Stephen Dunn and Toi Derricotte. For the next six years, I traveled in northern and central New Jersey, teaching writing in K-12 schools, welcoming spring flowers in the Garden State and trudging through dirty snow in Plainfield and Newark.

Each summer I ended up at the council's two week retreat at a Jersey college. There I witnessed the phenomenon of retreat breakdown. Some unstable art lover would have an episode, a "nervous breakdown" in the midst of scorching heat, freedom from mundane responsibility, and possibilities of epiphany through artistic creation.

old love

old love
when I approach you
even on paper pandora boxes
three thousand miles away
memories thrust in
to saturate my gaping
womanwound
rectifying urges surface
drown dowopdowop blues
I refuse him chocolate cake
infatuations transgress
saint mammy syndrome
salt pork shoppers starve
inward eyes   slow graying pubes
albert ayler recorded our song
heartloveheartlove died young
circular indecencies
exhume loud grapplings
in two family houses
our matrix held
we were synonymous
who believes it when it happens
babies scream in the night
people just want the bottle
why do I care if the sun don't shine
as long as I know he's mine
archie shepp lives on
off the radio
love plays
midcentury rage
loving eras record

paper love crumples

The trance of creative ferment fueled my writing.
Stephen, my perennial workshop leader, asked,
"What are you going to write about when you run
out of personal drama?" I had no answer for him. I
wasn't going to write marsh-and-pine-tree poems,
for heaven's sakes — I punched holes in the bottom
of my bank checks so they wouldn't clear too fast.
Sturm und Drang was my métier. Even when I
turned my inward gaze out, I caught drama, always
drama. A friend's broken heart led me straightaway
to blues:

Woman

I just want your pussy," so he said
and she presumed him better for the battering
of a 14-year bad marriage

> love puddle dry
> when the sun come out
> woman I just want your pussy

she saw him sweeter for the souring
and kinder for the harshening
and thus hungrier for her love

> heard folks marry
> till death do they part
> woman I just want your pussy

it seemed to go that way
until she turned a corner
and like stealth in a well-conceived plot

she came upon a thought (an infinite mistake
akin to weaving new blues
from a heart of deadred strings):

> gold disappear
> when the rainbow fade
> woman I just want your pussy

she would be sensitive to him
and he to her and they a one
the way pop tunes say love is done

but the boy who loved his old soul crooners
sang his song from the top of his shredded lung
in a howling wolf's voice:

> love puddle dry
> when the sun come out
> woman I just want your pussy

I grew apart from The Bergen Poets. I forgot their kindnesses though I kept in contact with Dorothy who was the Anne Sexton of the group – gifted, suffering mental illness and a crumbling marriage. She critiqued many of my poems that were later published. I drove her around and typed for her. When she was hospitalized in the county mental hospital, her palsy intensified. She moved to a care home.

When Alice, a Bergen poet and mother of eight, died from cancer, I saw my old buddies at her Catholic funeral. When the priest rotated Alice's casket, I got dizzy and mad at him for spinning her around so fast. It took me years to grasp that I was grieving not only Alice but my apprenticeship with the group.

Sometime later, John sat me down with the news that Dorothy, after smoking a last cigarette, walked into a lake—like Virginia Woolf—and drowned herself. The next two years were like a coda to my Jersey moment. My homing pigeon headed back to Oakland

the bus terminal

the missy children drop them off in
compact cars
they speak a different language
of cleaning
maiding
ironing
of pleasing me missus
of washing me missus tennis whites
of me missus children home for break
and extra loads to wash

turning out her very Jamaican lip one who
is young pouts
missy call her down during her favourite
show every time
will she have no peace from her missus?

rose barrette on plastic rose-coloured
stem sticks
in her hair
the weekend awaits its unburdening in
Brooklyn

the last maid in my line my grandmother
young
a chambermaid in a Muskogee hotel gingerly
picked up soiled towels shielding the pupils

of her young eyes from couples coupling
uncoupling
requesting fresh white towels her daughter told
me this young
teaching me to read and read well
so I'd never have this to fall back on

Cleaning Other People's Houses

When a friend asked me to join her condominium-cleaning business some years back, I recoiled. Moi? A black woman with degrees, fellowships, travels abroad, a library of dictionaries within my library—a cleaning woman? Cleaning other people's houses was necessity to my grandmothers, anathema to my mother and history to me. Was she out of her mind?

For certain black women, the Task is laid out early: get a good education, a good job; don't let any man bring you down; and don't look back. We're marched into society like toy soldiers to uphold the virtue of the race. When the mechanism runs down, the well-meaning elders who equipped us with our weapons of education, enunciation and etiquette are often several cities away.

Out of work, out of gas, going through a hellified midlife crisis, I had wearied of the Task. But, even in a breach, I was not supposed to clean toilets for a living. Loaded down with clients, my friend, a resilient, red-haired, onetime hippie, asked again. She and I had burned out as teachers. My funds narrowing, I accepted with a barrage of provisos: just for a while…just to see what it was like…until something better comes along.

For the next twenty months, we cleaned pricey condos in suburban New Jersey, luxury Siamese boxes with a sameness of design that made cleaning a matter of tactile geometry. My dismayed girlfriends, journalists and teachers all, suggested I incorporate, set up an agency for cleaning women, be a supplier of labor, not, for heaven's sake, the laborer herself.

Still, some fundamental, driving curiosity, and necessity, wouldn't let up. I fell back on it. The daughter who had been spared housework to do homework found cleaning other people's houses full of goalposts and tasks, the completion of which yielded immediate benefits. Shine, freshness, order and tranquility displaced metaphors, sestinas, end rhymes and point of view.

The experience had an adolescent tinge to it. With the music blasting and time sliding by in four-hour, eighty-dollar blocks, money piled up. As in adolescence, the goal was speed. Finish a condo, do a second, eat Tex-Mex, do a third. I learned shortcuts for every possible household chore.

Bathrooms and kitchens were singularly important.
Clients looked there to see their money's worth.
Getting the showers clean was sloppy at first.
Standing on rags and towels, we applied fabric soft-
ener (less toxic), rinsed it off, dried the surround,
and ended up sopping wet. Finally, we figured if we
cleaned the shower in the buff, our clothes would
stay dry and we wouldn't use up rags which we laun-
dered. Of course, one day, our psychiatrist-client
came home early. Marvin Gaye was blasting, the
water was running, the doctor was in his bedroom
before I knew it. I hollered, "Don't come in!" When
I came out, I let him know exactly how we got his
glass shower to sparkle. He seemed amused.

Typically, our mostly male clients never saw us.
Bachelors, divorced men, gay couples, widowers,
they left early or were away on business for days at
a time. I liked cleaning their houses, polishing their
mirrors, turning on their superior sound systems,
and dusting and bopping my way through their cool
environments. Instead of the forced voyeurism I had
heard about, I discovered an inverted voyeurism, an
intimacy minus the intimate. I was inside their lives;
their lives were inside mine. I knew which deodorant they used, which sections of the paper they
treasured, the radio stations they listened to, the
real color of their hair, the amount of liquor they
consumed, their taste in books.

I found these forays into the male domain like
simulated wife maneuvers. It should have been no
surprise that I had more problems with women,
especially those who had difficulty relinquishing
dominion. There were those who couldn't leave
the room, let alone the house, while we were in it.
Those didn't last long. One woman had her toddler

present me with the day's pay, crumpled and sweaty. The second time it happened, I told her off. "This is beneath demeaning. You're saying, in effect, that my coming here cleaning your house is child's play?" She half-apologized, the old dodge — "I'm sorry if I offended you." But we had more business than we could handle. It was refreshing to flounce my black ass out of there only pausing to say, "You're going to have to find somebody else." Oh my, I fired her.

I think it was harder for women to pay for a service they traditionally provided free, as an unspoken stipulation of the marriage contract. It was also harder for some women clients to accept that their houses needed extra cleaning, i.e. extra money, whereas the men wanted the work done and us out of there when they got home…period.

The home of an interracial, professional gay couple was my favorite. The black man, Ron, had an arresting blow-up of his grandfather upstairs; its piercing eyes followed me as I dusted and vacuumed. I found myself asking his portrait questions, giving rejoinders, packing whole histories of my life into twenty-minute conversations.

One week, I couldn't help notice a book about AIDS on the nightstand. As weeks went by, more books appeared. My friend and I speculated over lunch as to which one was sick. It didn't take long to discover that Ron was in an advanced stage. I got used to his being home, the clink of his spoon as he ate ice cream, the way he padded from room to room as we cleaned, switching on cable news.

The grandfather's gaze encompassed my feelings, an array that surfaced involuntarily as the illness progressed. I felt reproach, anger, sorrow, anguish.

One day, I came downstairs, my "dialogue" finished for the day. I walked into the living room and recognized instantly the two women there as Ron's mother and sister. Their physical similarity to the gruff grandfather was softened by their protective stances. We stood there, a strange familiarity between us, this gay man, his family and me. Little in our upbringing had given us sight of these eventualities, that he would be openly gay, that they would be supportive as he died of AIDS, that I would be his Beulah.

Whenever I ran into problems, cleaning or otherwise, I fell back on the great rhetorical "Why am I here?" Testing my strength against that of my ancestors? Tackling a horrific job that no one should ever have to do? I knew it was temporary, and it wasn't horrific, just tedious and inglorious.

One afternoon, a wife of a cardiologist was reduced to tears because a neighbor had snubbed her. Politely, I offered sympathy, but I thought her sheltered, self-absorbed, spoiled. She constantly offered me lunch. I refused. I was intent on finishing her three-story townhouse in six hours. She offered more money because her place was larger. I accepted. Gradually we got to know each other, shared experiences in mothering, growing up, romance, grad school. It turned out we were both doctoral dropouts. I found out she was a wonderful cook; she learned I had read at her YWHA and asked to see my poetry. When she cried again, I could not dismiss her tears as trivial. I could no longer dismiss her point of view or her frame of reference.

I have never looked at myself as much as I did during those months of cleaning. Mirrors were everywhere. I began to see my life clearly, even starkly. In a pique, I quit one week and found work as an office temp at one-third the pay. The supervisor kept calling me Bertha ("I'm sorry, you look like a Bertha.") I stuck it out for four days before heading back to condo country where nobody called me Bertha, Beulah or Bessie.

I found out how strong I was, mentally and physically, after all those hours of bending, squatting, twisting, elbowing, polishing and emptying. However strong a mind I possessed, though, my body couldn't take it. My back, always strong, began to ache.

One morning, a fiftyish matron insisted that we sit and discuss *The Color Purple* which she had just finished reading. We talked about the horror and beauty in Alice Walker's vision. The irony of our discussion didn't escape me. Alice Walker had championed Zora Neale Hurston, the novelist-folklorist of the Harlem Renaissance who had spent her last impoverished decade as a domestic in Florida.

I didn't last much longer. The experiment was over.

Not long after, I passed a woman, black like me, carrying her plastic bags into a subdivision lined with three-story colonials. I felt a mixture of empathy, relief and gratitude. With no alternative choices or yuppie townhouses to "lite" clean, I suspect her working conditions were much harsher than mine had been. Cleaning other people's houses was her necessity, and, for a time, it had been my necessity too. Doing her job helped me cross the threshold of middle-age. Cleaning other people's houses had made my own life habitable again.

A Playwright-in-progress

I was a fellow in the Robert Frierson Playwriting Workshop at the Lorraine Hansberry Theatre (LHT) in San Francisco in 1991 when I learned some golden lessons about myself and writing. My journaling helped me understand that:

- I learn through making big, fat mistakes vs. reading/perfecting in my mind.

- The main trade secret I keep getting is that theater operates as a closed shop, but the one (other) entry is perfected skill.

- My main reason for taking so many workshops is to keep writing.

- I'm trying to see where I should put my primary emphasis—poetry, fiction, or plays.

- Oh boy, writers need support systems badly.

- Being mentored by extraordinary people is a strong theme in my work and life.

Stanley, the head of LHT, came in the first night and spoke to the fellows. He shook the guys' hands and not mine. I was the only woman present. He avoided my eyes and couldn't remember my name. I seemed to recall this kind of chummy clique-y attitude in theater before. Circles are closed until you break through. Our "esteemed" playwright-leader R. hardly talked about tonight's subject — plot and structure. Instead he sounded on how he hadn't gotten paid yet from LHT. When Stanley left, he and the others dissed him. So, the men didn't like him either…Next week: two more women…a relief…Stanley ignored me again. He spoke to the other women… maybe he's not a misogynist…I noticed one thing about this workshop which was so hard to get in, so very very selective: it wasn't making me productive…Nina, the sculptor, and I talked a lot because we were always on time and R. late. I liked her. She was from the Midwest, like my college roomie. I love Midwesterners. I connect with their dry humor. …R. talked about the Henry Tanner play he was writing…I liked that he gave up a lot of information about the theater. He deglamorized it. When he got the SF Bay Guardian award, he was driving a cab — one cliché I never want to experience. Cleaning condos for two years was enough for my bones. R. and my previous playwriting instructor quoted Lagos Egri like his book was the Bible. I read it but it was hard for me to grasp.

I learn through doing and making mistakes vs. reading and perfecting in my mind…Finally they got to my play. I'd been so selfish and self-absorbed. I only read Nina's and Mike's…The plays by Susan and Nate, the other two, I couldn't read with great interest; I picked them up and put them down unaffected. I missed class (flu) when they did Susan's. I liked her and would have hated to comment on her work…She'd been kicking around in costume design for 10 years professionally. She was from

Spelman College, the Vassar of the Black colleges. She wanted to be called by Hollywood and bitched about the $300 budget from Stanley. Did anybody like this guy? I got tons of suggestions — really explicit — on my play. Once home, I saw that Nate hated it. That hurt. I took his copy out the next day and studied it. Next class, he said, "I have real problems with this play," but said he had written them down and it wasn't necessary to go over them twice. Everybody's eyebrows rose. He didn't like the play or me. P. was our guest playwright. Boy, was he interesting. A real careerist in a laid back, surefooted way. Talk about being right person, right place, right time for Asian work. He was the one. Interesting to hear him and R. talk about LA theatre scene…so much is dependent on knowing the right person who likes your work/you. The chummies. On balance, this workshop was more discouraging than not.

The main trade secret I keep getting is that theatre is a closed shop but that the one entry is through perfected skill. We went for drinks, all of us, afterward. That helped; liquor loosens things. P. spoke bluntly about being a token; let's not fool ourselves, he said. The conversation got a bit tight as P. revealed he'd gotten some of that screenwriting money that R. was always talking about. So many branches in the writing world, I don't know where to perch. Seems like a man's world to me — maybe that's why the fem/lesbians decided to go off and do their own thing.

So many branches in the writing world —
I don't know where to perch

My main reason for taking so many workshops is to keep writing. But my strategy didn't work with LHT; I needed feedback, not just weekly schmoozing. If I'm writing 20-page chapters for the novel or six-page scenes, I'm happy. If not, I'm not...I went to see R.'s play at The Herbst. The Abe Lincoln Brigade, old line Berkeley radicals of the folk singing variety, filled the place for a benefit. It was like a step back in time with the play being *Uncle Tom's Cabin* in modernist take. It was interesting. Very clumsily-acted in parts. I sat behind R. The play was stridently polemical, melodramatic, but it worked. I determined to learn how to use melodrama. I don't want to write a thinky play. R. grumbled that the Tanner play only had one technical run through. He was pissed at Stanley for that. He said two checks from the SF Mime Troupe bounced also. I got a negative sensation in my gut. He'd been doing this shtick, winning prizes, getting plays on the black experience mounted since 1979 but seemed stuck on a career ladder with the waning black theater vogue. Was this where I was headed? Bounced checks and writing plays for silver-haired radicals?

I'm really trying to see where I should put my primary emphasis — poetry, fiction, or playwriting. I'm not young; I have to make some decisions at this intersection. Writing has been a delicious buffet as I've sampled poetry, fiction and playwriting. I need to "go all the way" with one but wondered if I can. Am I just a big enthusiast with varied talents? R. was doing a play on Huey P. Newton and the party. Since I was a Panther and we'd talked about it before, he wanted to pick my brains. "I wasn't in on the big stuff. I was behind-the-scenes." *I'm picking my own brains, Buster. Go find another brain to pick.* I feel like I'll never get anything of substance from him — and I like him. He's funny and touching but struggling just like I am. Only he's had umpteen productions. What's it all about, Alfie? **Oh boy, writers need support systems badly.** I worked hard and brought in a scene. R. is remodeling his house (money must've been coming in from somewhere) and so busy all he did was jaw on the remodel. Somebody else would've called this sexist, that he always has his own concerns primary. And there is a sexual undercurrent between us that I try to ignore. I heard LHT had to almost shut down, and maybe wouldn't have our staged readings at all. Strangely, this is a relief. Do I need a reading under these circumstances? *Why aren't I more enthusiastic about this reading? For starters, how about — I have some standards of my own. I'm not just a fish out here to be flipped around.* As things begin to wrap on the fellowship, I'm trying to be positive and put playwriting in a proper perspective. What did I get? What did I lose? I go to the last workshop out of sorts. Too many balls juggling my other manuscripts; and again, am I going to have to choose between fiction, poetry and playwriting? I make a big flub and forget the main character in someone's play. The writer looks at me, aghast, then quickly regroups and the conversation goes on.

The women artists I encountered were hardworking, self-sacrificing, generous, often defiantly unhappy and did their own shitwork.

77

Burn out. From there on out, I was fishing in my own jumbled insides. I needed renewal. I'd lost motivation. I was getting sick. LHT called to say the readings were on. The manuscript was not done. It was hard to rev back up. I called LHT. Got my deadline extended. When the staged reading did go up, it was — surprise, surprise — well-attended, 60+ people. A lively discussion. Afterwards, I waited for weeks for a nibble, a crumb, anything. Stanley called — the play would go forward. He gave me a date. Sure enough, my play, my very own play, got advance mention in *The San Francisco Chronicle* Datebook. At my next meeting with Stanley, I brought up payment, compensation, moolah. He said the budget was tight, tight, tight. "But I will be paid something?" He jumped up from the table and threw my precious script down, getting loud and funky. "I made Ntozake Shange. How dare you question me!" I yelled back, "You have to pay me something. What are you saying? Not even carfare from across the Bay." He stormed out. I didn't know what to think except crazy. Two days later, he left a phone message: LHT was pulling the production because of lack of funds. I went back to the novel, a coming-of-age story, after cursing out my telephone answering machine.

Ironically being mentored by extraordinary people is a strong theme in my work. I have been exposed to a colorful lot of male writers and artists, putative fathers who showed me their discipline and craft. I absorbed my lessons while assisting, chauffeuring, transcribing, interviewing, opening for, cleaning house or buying groceries for The Artist, witnessing all manner of excess — alcoholics, egomaniacs, dissolutes, self-centered pricks, fame hounds, leeches, misogynists, stuffed shirts, wife abusers and serial adulterers.

Because of that exposure I kept ideas of a full-fledged artistic career at arms length for many years. I thought that the horrid qualities invariably came with great and even not-so-great accomplishment.

The women artists I encountered were hardworking, self-sacrificing, generous, and often defiantly unhappy, and they did their own shitwork. Although they seemed to be happier once they achieved a certain level of success and financial independence, I concluded early on that being an artist was damaging to one's own life and to loved ones. Reading about the writers of the Harlem Renaissance, watching and reading Beat and post-Beat writers, befriending the writers of the black arts movement in the 1960s/70s, I repressed my artistic ambitions—fascinated, terrified, humbled by their commitment and passion, horrified by the sacrifice, chaos and suffering of their loved ones.

Perhaps I was simply an impressionable young person. I had come, after all, from a strict religious family. The imbalance in my family of origin, my mother, in my mind, turning whole-hog to religion as a salve for my father's compulsive gambling, triggered my susceptibility to being disillusioned by any pseudo-parents. It took a while to find the parent in myself, to rephrase Ntozake Shange's "I found God in myself" from *for colored girls who have considered suicide/when the rainbow is enuf*.

It took time to acquire the wisdom that experience brings. Once I got it, I understood how to live a balanced life **and** pursue writing.

Putting the Funny in the Novel

*All through his twenties, I congratulated my son
for not making me a grandma. Like I thought that was
birth control. When he hit 30, I shut up because
I was afraid I'd never become a grandma. I guess I
threw away The Pill. He had a son at 32.*

Sitting across from me in his favorite San Francisco
restaurant, my agent—white and erudite— thumped
my novel manuscript, and said, "How come the
humor in your conversation isn't here on the page?"
I was writing about the harrowing experiences
of becoming a Black Panther in the sixties in San
Francisco. Not exactly a fount of funny, I thought.

His favorite dish, the one he urged me to order,
shrimp scampi with linguini, suddenly tasted papery.
People routinely laughed at my takes on politics, sex,
menopause and post menopause, being black, getting old while being black. My sense of humor is a
survival skill. Surely I could put funny in the novel.

I was determined to figure this out—how to get the
humor that spilled from my mouth into my novel.
I've always loved comedians. I saw Richard Pryor
when he was a young comic at The Purple Onion in
the city. My secret fantasy had long been to perform
as a comic. If that would put my manuscript over
the top I'd try it.

When my son's girlfriend had her baby shower, I found
out I wasn't a grandma. I was the babydaddymomma.
Even so, I was proud. Then I went to buy a stroller and
got sticker shock. It cost more than I paid for my first car.

I come from a long line of gabbers, but the performers I knew best were the preachers of my childhood—bombastic in their regal robes, kings of the church who had women, banquets, love offerings, parsonages provided without question. One famous local evangelist was rumored to have bitten off the nipple of a loving underage suppliant. Another beat his wife so severely the domestic abuse charges made the local papers. And, of course, I am from Oakland, the home of His Grace King Narcisse, he of the red-velvet ministry and Rolls-Royce flamboyance. As a daughter of a longtime church secretary, I heard it all—firsthand, secondhand, through rumors, gossip and innuendo. As an adolescent, I found it comical as well as disgraceful. Witnessing hypocrisy cultivated a sharp cynicism.

I saw Billy Graham on TV. He looked like
Frankenstein. Face bloated, clothes too big. I had
to Google him to make sure he was still alive.
Where were his handlers? I wanted to shout at them:
Look up! Look at the monitor! Stop counting
the money! Fix him!!

When I joined the civil rights movement—the radical end through the black student movement and Black Panthers—I saw again the inner workings of a large social phenomenon and the contradictions between conviction and faith, privilege and sexism. My novel, *Virgin Soul*, explores the gradual radicalization of a young black woman in the midst of these contradictions. Humor was not my objective although my girlfriends and I — barely out of our teens — laughed our way through the violence, threats to our lives from police, the FBI, the agent provocateurs, and our own carelessness. It would take decades for me to understand that our silliness, giggles, and elbow poking at the outrageousness we witnessed protected us. I still had to figure out where the funny would come from — or, at least, how to tread that line between the comic and painful.

Using the local free papers, I found the underground comedy scene and made my way to the Brainwash Café. There I met a Bay Area legend, host/comic Tony Sparks. I went to his drop-a-buck-in-the-cup venues. The Tuesday one started around 7pm. I was so unsure of myself that I'd wait until the room cleared and get up around 9:30 in front of the diehards.

It took me six weeks of going to the comedy venues to get a laugh. When I asked Tony's advice, he commented that people listened to me intently because I was aging. Distressed, I repeated that and he shook his head: "I said it's because you're *engaging*." He then suggested that I keep using narratives but inject punch lines every few sentences. I took the advice and started getting consistent laughs.

Ants drive me nuts! They're so systematic...like armies. I think they have dictators, just like people, who send the little brown ants, the babies first—kind of like the Palestinians, young women and children first.

The world of comedy intrigued me. I never did a pratfall on stage, but, in the Tenderloin, passing by a bunch of drug dealers and dope heads, I tripped and my straw bag spilled out wallet, prescription drugs, loose change, and notebooks. I skinned my knee, so scared I didn't know what to do. Everyone eagerly helped me. When I got to the comedy venue, I checked and my stuff was all there.

The babydaddy, my son, and the babymomma told me they had decided not to use the n-word around my grandson. The next time I had him, he said dammit every time he got frustrated. When they picked him up, I said, "Which one of you African-Americans uses dammit in front of him?"

I saw progress. I got to a one-woman show by a comic friend of Tony's. I entered the 3rd floor of a building in the Castro. It was pitch dark; I fell over drums and tympani that made a loud sound. I expected the noise to alert someone to help me. No one came. I sat there in the dark until I pulled it together. When I went in, I saw why no one came out. There were only two people in the audience. Even though the solitary actor was dreadfully unfunny, I laughed to support her. Funny takes a lot of nerve, I was finding out.

Black people have a disease called "I don't wanna work for the man" and another disease — namebranditis. When these two diseases come together, it's called "Broke."

I didn't understand why the comics did the same routine over and over for weeks until I learned they were working on the timing. Later, I saw two of them on *Last Comic Standing*, doing the exact same routines to great laughs. I recalled seeing Richard Pryor in his final public performance at The Circle

Star Theater in San Carlos, dozing off onstage and working the hell out of a 20 minute set, his wheelchair and onstage nurse as much prop as medical necessity.

I was married for 11 years. So I identify with prisoners. And who made marriage a gruesome marathon — "till death do us part"?

When I brought a big white vibrator with a purple head to the Brainwash, I got more laughs than ever and provided everyone who followed me with material. I see why prop comics go straight to Vegas.

I decide to bring my funny to a notoriously hard venue in Oakland. Luenell, who would grab her 15-minutes in *Borat,* hosts. One night, drunk, she moons the crowd, pulling her pants down and showing her big yellow backside to one and all. I don't go on that night. I come another week and do a short set that bombs. In the middle of it, Luenell shouts, "You going over the head of these first-of-the-month nigguhs." Another night, I do a successful bit on a black TV evangelist but make the mistake of inviting a favorite cousin who is a pastor. It gets laughs but not from her.

I finally get a paying gig when Tony invites me to a venue in Emeryville, a town next door to Oakland. I'm scared but bring a set list of bits that I keep going over during the evening. The feisty woman headliner takes one look at me and says, "Oh hell no!" Tony lets me know I'm out and apologizes, but says I can sit at the comics' table and get free drinks. She ignores me but starts a rant: "I hate people who come out once a week and have the nerve to call themselves comedians." She's out five nights a week, she says, sometimes hitting two or three spots a night. I'm coming out maybe once a month at that point. She works the craft of comedy the way I work the craft of writing.

My son, like the comedienne, can't believe I'm doing this. "Mom, you're not a comic. You're funny. Sometimes." They're both right. In trying to put the funny in my work, I discover my humor and sarcasm spring from the eruptions of irony in my daily life. I'm not a comic; I'm an ironist, an observational ironist. I venture closer to my novel's subject matter, being a young black militant in the 60s.

I was in the Black Panther Party as a teenager. For heaven's sake, they welcomed white people. Out of all the militant groups, they welcomed white people with open arms. Armed with .357 magnums.

I realize that I'm not going to inject funny into my novel, any more than I can make shrimp scampi my favorite dish; my romance with comedy ends and I return to editing the manuscript. The writing becomes tighter and, in some way, laced with a deeper irony.

The N-word: Let's not throw out the baby with the bathwater

What will it take for this dreaded, haunted, innuendo-filled word to become a relic, a fossil, a member in good standing of the word museum?

I.

In August Wilson's Pulitzer Prize-winning play "Fences," I heard James Earl Jones thunder the word over and over at the 46th Street Theater in New York in 1987. My sister and I sat in front of a vocal sistuh whose obnoxious commentary rattled us. At the climax, the garbage man Trey (Jones) brings home his outside baby to his long suffering wife, his outside woman having died in childbirth. When Jones walked on, baby in his arms, the sistuh hollered, "Oh, no, he didn't." The great thespian James Earl Jones broke the fourth wall and glared at me. I felt like I could clock the sistuh, but that would've been pointless.

Wilson's 28 uses of the N-word in "Fences" are anything but pointless. They are signifying of the highest order. Troy, the garbage man whose plight is the heart of the play, never addresses his wife Rose with it, only his sons and buddy Bono whom he met in prison. The volatile word doesn't appear in the various work songs, secular chants, and field hollers in the play. But Wilson opens the play with it:

BONO: Troy, you ought to stop that lying!

TROY: I ain't lying! The nigger had a watermelon this big....Talking about ... "What watermelon, Mr. Rand?" I liked to fell out! "What watermelon, Mr. Rand...And it sitting there big as life."

BONO: What did Mr. Rand say?

TROY: Ain't said nothing. Figure if the nigger too dumb to know he carrying a watermelon, he wasn't gonna get much sense out of him. Afraid to let the white man see him carry it home.

From the jump Troy is smart and knows it. A smart garbage man. A smart black garbage man in 1957. He uses the N-word repeatedly in camaraderie, where it is a term of endearment ("I love you, nigger"), gossip, history ("I done seen a hundred niggers play baseball better than Jackie Robinson."), and definition by appositive ("If I had all the money niggers, these Negroes, throw away on numbers for one week—just one week—I'd be a rich man."). Bono only utters it twice, each time admonishing Troy about his hardheadedness.

In its final appearance in the play, the N-word holds intimacy and anonymity in the same breath. Troy kicks his son Cory him out of the house: "Nigger! That's what you are. You just another nigger on the street to me!" The word is the blues, and Troy is the blues, a man who hates that he's "been standing in the same place for eighteen years." Devalued by Rose who agrees to raise the child but forsakes him ("From right now...this child got a mother. But you a womanless man"), Troy becomes a defeated man, the blues personified, what he called his son—"just another nigger on the street."

Houston A. Baker Jr. defines Afro-American culture as a "complex, reflexive enterprise which finds its proper figuration in blues conceived of as matrix… …a womb, a network…. Afro-American blues constitute such a vibrant network…They are the multiplex, enabling script in which Afro-American cultural discourse is inscribed."[1]

It is impossible to remove the N-word from this matrix, from the blues, from the vast "enabling script in which Afro-American cultural discourse is inscribed." And one might as well confess, from American cultural discourse. Even if banished from conversation, one would have to 1) censor myriad texts from several centuries, 2) discard rap which, in itself, is providing a valuable history of Afro-American culture and discourse, and 3) perform mind control on millions of people.

While writing this essay, I saw "Fences" in Mill Valley, California, with the magnificent actor Carl Lumbly ("Alias") playing Troy. I'd forgotten how the play starts with that jocular N-word exchange between Troy and Bono. But Lumbly's woebegone Troy thwarted the N-word's nastiness. Instead I felt the loss of solace in Troy's world, his diminution and slow death as the fence got built. Weeks later, I counted the number of times the word appeared in the play.

[1] Baker, Jr., Houston A. *Blues, Ideology, and Afro-American Literature: A Vernacular Theory.* Chicago: University of Chicago Press, 1987.

II.

I still use the N-word. I relish hearing it come out
of my mouth in intimate conversation. My closest
friends use the word around me. I have used it selec-
tively around certain white friends (who don't dare
use it in my presence). I would like to say I don't use
it around strangers, children and babies. But I've
used it around strangers in standup routines and
later while reading my novel *Virgin Soul* across the
country since March 2012. I've been taken aback by
how harsh the N-word sounds when spoken aloud
in a public library, how cool it sounds in a nightclub
or a jazz setting, how petrifying it sounded at my
local college library, where I could've heard a pin
drop, none of the guffawing within the other relaxed
environments (with drinks flowing freely).

Virgin Soul took repeated drafts to get the novel
right, and one complete draft to eliminate excessive
use of the N-word which I couldn't do away with.
Virgin Soul being historical fiction, the N-word at
points lent authenticity. I self-censored because
of the forced extinction and burial of the N-word
with which I agree, in part. Used with the threat
and/or act of murder, discrimination, prejudice, or
brutality, of course the N-word is an abominable
travesty. Used with affection between friends, in
the height of lovemaking (yeah, people get freaky
with it), when making an emphatic point in dialogue between podnahs, e.g. at a barbershop, on a
street corner, at a family dinner with the o.g.'s in the
family a little toasted, the N-word is appropriate.

I hate that police use it against black men, and
it has become acceptable, expected and not even
expounded upon by either party. No one seems to

recognize the enormously intimate relationship between white cops and black suspects (who often then become victims, convicts or recidivists). For hundreds of years now, this closeness, this Cain-and-Abel relationship, has flourished here in the United States. Nowhere else like it does here. We've permitted a special closeness between black people and armed white men in uniforms, whether they're called police, National Guard, transit cops, prison guards or patrollers. Think of it. Who else can hit you about your head, limbs or torso, causing contusions, curse you, call you every name in the book including the N-word, and then tell you to call your lawyer? The only other person I've known who can get away with that is a husband. It is accepted, expected and procedural. Oh, husbands can't hit wives, you say. Police don't abuse suspects and reality is a rainbow. You wish. You can tell me to stop using the N-word all you want, but I never physically assault my friends when I use the word. I never beat them to the musical accompaniment of the N-word in two-beat chords. I'm very cordial and explanatory when I use the word, even anecdotally, with carefully chosen whites.

In teaching college literature for the past two decades, I've had two times when the N-word caused discomfort. The first occurred when my English literature class read aloud Flannery O'Connor's "A Good Man Is Hard to Find." The protagonist in this short story, a grandmother traveling in 1940s Georgia, sees a backwoods black child whom she calls a "cute little pickaninny." When her granddaughter sees he doesn't even have pants on, the grandmother says, "(L)ittle niggers in the country don't have the things we do."

At this point, a black student got up and walked out of my class. She said she wouldn't put up with black people being referred to this way. She never came back. This was midway through a 4-unit class, nothing to sneeze at. But the rest of the class had a lively discussion that day that brought out a lot of wisdom and understanding.

More recently, my English Lit class read aloud August Wilson's "Fences" in a circle, a common technique for teaching plays. Three or four students read a scene, the next three or four students in the circle read the next scene, and so on, more random than casting for type. The day we read it, in a three-hour seminar, several students had a chance to read Troy's lines. A white male student read Troy's part, and class ended without time for a discussion. On the way home, I was perturbed. That last student reading a barrage of the N-word echoed in my head. His inflections sounded horrible, harsh and ugly, instead of familiar and affectionate. The next class I spoke about my reaction. We went back to the play and had several students of different races read the same lines with the N-word. The students agreed that the word sounded different but they hadn't my extreme reaction. One explained that they knew the word sounded different when different kinds of people said it. They pretty much concluded that it sounded white and not intimate when spoken by one not so in tune with black culture, but defended each other's attempt to capture August Wilson's meaning, regardless of the N-word's explosive possibility within the currency of the day.

The first classroom incident upset a student but not me, the second upset me but not the students. Words can be land mines, lethal and dangerous, or

simply signs that tell people what's ahead. Using the
N-word in literature, though, after its burial by the
NAACP, its use by J-Lo that led to a proposed boy-
cott, and its NFL ban, is even trickier than students
discovering it in the canon. But it's not impossible
for this word to become a relic. Other words have
become fossils, like malagrugorous (dismal) or jar-
gogle (to confuse). People don't twist their mouths
to say these words because they've been in the word
museum for centuries.

Do we want to censor John Langston Gwaltney's
moving history of ordinary black people in his
anthropological book *Drylongso: A Self-Portrait
of Black America* because of the N-word?

> "But if I show my black face in certain
> places, every cop in creation is right
> there." "What is your business here?"
> "Keep moving, nigger." "Do you
> work for some white family around
> here?" "Shit, this might just as soon
> be South Africa."

If we cut the N-word here, as some want done to
Huckleberry Finn, we remove the historical record of
its use. If we censor comics using the word, we drive
the impulse to say and hear it underground where
it joins the black market (pun intended). It took me
years to read Paul Lawrence Dunbar without disgust, and, similarly, old sayings like this one:

> White man got de money an' education.
> De Nigguh got Gawd an' conjuration.

Was it the conflation of the N-word with dialect or my disgust which obscured the insight that "Gawd an' conjuration" enabled black people to survive their holocaust?

III.

I'm actually not one to address my son with the N-word. Nor did my mother, a proper Oklahoman, ever use the word in direct address. But she quoted my grandmother, with relish, who forbade her daughters to party with "roundhouse niggers at the juke joint" in Muskogee, Oklahoma. My grandmother was steering posterity in a right direction. When my son began seeing a young woman with an adorable son while we (the village) were tending to his own adorable son, I pulled on the blunter part of my grandma's wisdom to make myself abundantly clear: "Son, we not raising yo' baby while you go off and raise some other nigger's baby. Let him raise his son and you raise yours."

If brothers were in my audience at the Brainwash Café & Laundromat, a comedy spot in San Francisco, they would call out: "Do the black man fucking routine." I could do it, i.e. use the N-word, because I was Troy Maxson talking to my homies. If it was mostly or only whites, using the N-word would have been degradation. Depending on how late it was, how raucous it was, how many blacks were there, I used the politically incorrect version. Call it the Dave Chappelle Syndrome. Dave quit his $50-mill gig when his comedy crossed the line between satire and self-abnegation.

(The politically incorrect version)

Nigguhs get ferocious when they fuck Cuz nigguhs gotta represent when they make love. They gotta represent their family, other black men, all your past lovers— they bring all that into the bed. So please do not attempt to fuck a bro on a futon. You see Hollywood shows you how white men fuck ON TABLES & STAIRS & HARD SURFACES, ON DESKS & MARBLE STAIRCASES. Please!! This is not black men.

They need air bags underneath, not just mattresses. SPHLAT!! To fuck a black man, you need air bags, mattresses, foam, waterbeds, Sealy Posturepedic. And you best have a chiropractor in the next room. Nigguhs work at fucking. Some may say *fuck work but they work hard at fucking.*

Now, try the same routine with *brothers, bro,* or *men* in place of the N-word. It's called censorship or language manipulation. Controversial words stay alive and kicking because they have multiple meanings according to their use and their users. I'm not indifferent to arguments against the N-word. But I know, as a black person, that satirical comments and sarcasm about race are an intramural sport for black people. They offset the destructive and unrelenting racism that is the American way of life. Black writers, comics and social commentators get enormous mileage and ducats from acerbic satire. We will get to a post racist planet someday, maybe from a solar system where we can watch ourselves play with unkindness.

I heard a white TV actress say, "I feel vibratious." I hope she was nervous and not just simple. When Dubya was the country's father, he repeatedly said "nukaleer" instead of nuclear. He wasn't impeached for that because it wasn't a crime. Sarah Palin commits linguistic abomination every time she speaks. But because she doesn't curse and looks like a 1950s Bess Myerson/Miss America, she's indulged. I can hardly listen to Al Sharpton without calling up a friend to repeat his latest malapropism. I can't act like the N-word is the worst crime against society. When it's part of a crime, then it's part of a crime. But when Weezy told George Jefferson on *The Jeffersons,* "Nigga, pullease," that was as important as the signing of the Magna Carta. That was one for the books. The N-word can be horrible. It can be humorous. It has the duplicity of the f-word.

A terrible homicide in Oakland led me to the prose poem "Bruno was from Brazil." I dared to satirize *nigger* in print because neither its commonplace use, nor its uncommon power or simple banishment will eradicate the cancer in race relations in this country. It's not problem or solution; it's an indication.

Bruno was from Brazil: a prose poem

"I'm from Oakland and I'm not a statistic. Yet.
But New Year's Eve I left the Bank of America
at 2:30pm; the news that night flashed on my
bank. It was the scene of the last homicide
of the year, at 3:20pm, which meant I dodged
a bullet by about 45 minutes. Witnesses say
two Latino males and two African-American
males had a parking lot altercation. The Latino
driver used an ethnic slur and one of the black
guys pulled out a gun and shot him. The two
blacks drove off, witnesses say, and Bruno who
was from Brazil and delivered pizza, for god's
sake, died on the spot…now you know the
last word in the guidebook for new arrivals is
nigger. And I know poor, poor Bruno heard the
word a thousand times delivering those pizzas.
'Some nigguz on 90th Ave. want mushroom/
salami/chicken…only nigguz want combos like
that…you my nigga…when you get money
from nigguz, check for counterfeit…nigguz,
Bruno, watch out…' Poor Bruno, the word
probably came off his tongue like spit. And he
didn't know you could call a black person a
nigger and get utter scorn and contempt. Like
down South where they just ignored it and
kept their inner dignity. But Bruno, you don't
call a real nigga a nigga. That's like a death wish.
Are you crazy? Suicidal? Certain words are like
gods. They command respect. Nigger is a god.
I'm so sorry for Bruno. He was a sacrificial
lamb—that's what you have to do with gods.
You have to appease them, give em a lil' somepin somepin. And I know Richard Pryor went to
Africa after he made $50 million off the word

and came back with religion. Stopped using the word and used crack instead. But he didn't stop folks from using it. He just made the word an academic issue: *shall we nigger; shall we not nigger?* Forget Dick Gregory's autobiography called Nigger. No, a Harvard law professor writes a book called *Nigger: The Strange Career of a Troublesome Word.* Nigger is a God, nigger made millions, now it has a career. And the country's leading black intellectual, a guy named Skippy, finds one of the first novels written by a black, titled, what else, *Our Nig.* So I'm proposing a constitutional amendment on the use of the word. There are simply days when it is dangerous to use the word. And one of those days is Friday night. And another of those days is Saturday night. Ok? On MLK's birthday, abstain. Christmas, it goes without saying. The season is the reason. And proceed with caution on the Fourth of July. Fireworks, drinking and the use of the word by the wrong people don't mix."

APPENDIX I

A Critique of "Bruno Was From Brazil" by
Jendi Reiter[1]

This month's unusual and provocative piece, "Bruno
Was From Brazil" by Judy Juanita, crosses the
boundaries of genre (appropriately for a poem about
explosive cross-cultural interaction). An example of
the fluid form known as the prose poem, which has
become increasingly popular in literary journals, this
piece would also work well as a slam poetry performance. Neither form can rely on line breaks to
signify that the text is "poetic", forcing the author
to pay closer attention to aural patterns and timing
in order to give the piece the musical momentum
and intensity of a poem. Writing prose poems, or
reading one's work aloud, are both useful tools for
free-verse poets to discover whether they are allowing line breaks to substitute for true poetic speech.

What exactly is a prose poem? This overview from
the Academy of American Poets website notes:
"While it lacks the line breaks associated with
poetry, the prose poem maintains a poetic quality, often utilizing techniques common to poetry,
such as fragmentation, compression, repetition, and
rhyme." Juanita's poem fits this description, with
its staccato sentences, its wide-ranging associative
leaps between topics and varieties of diction (news
reports, conversation, academese and slang), and
especially its mesmerizing repetition of That Word.

"Bruno Was From Brazil" initially leans toward
the prosy side of the equation, beginning in the
voice of a hard-boiled detective story: "I'm from

[1] Reprinted by permission of Jendi Reiter. http://winningwriters.com/
resources/bruno-was-from-brazil

Oakland and I'm not a statistic. Yet." Halfway through, somewhere around the line "Certain words are like gods," the piece takes off as a manic riff on racially charged language and whether its sting can ever be dulled by context. Without line breaks (brakes?), the words spill out furiously, defying decorum and step-by-step logic, so that when we finally reach the author's satirical "solution" of a constitutional amendment, it's obvious that we'll never be able to draw neat lines separating safe from dangerous uses of the word. In this way, the author's chosen form enhances the message and emotional impact of her story.

The hybrid poetic form liberates Juanita to include sentences that would feel too wordy and technical in a traditional lyric poem (particularly the section from "Forget Dick Gregory's autobiography" to "Our Nig"). Other sentences, by contrast, display more of the aphoristic, non-literal qualities of poetry: "now you know the last word in the guidebook for new arrivals is nigger"; "Stopped using the word and used crack instead"; and the passage "Certain words are like gods. They command respect. Nigger is a god. I'm so sorry for Bruno. He was a sacrificial lamb—that's what you have to do with gods. You have to appease them, give em a lil' somepin somepin."

The repetition of the word "god" parallels the subsequent variations on "nigger", reinforcing the connection between these concepts. Gods are lethally unpredictable, a power that we try and fail to contain with words and rituals, and yet a power we can't resist invoking to make sense of our lives. This poem suggests that racial and cultural identity, and perhaps even language itself, are essential aspects of being human, but also have the potential to dehumanize. Where there are borders, there will be wars.

The latter half of the poem seems to deride academic efforts to domesticate the word, implicitly questioning whether this is just another way of encouraging children to play with live ammunition. The line between safe and unsafe contexts is easy to cross unawares; wouldn't it be better to suppress the word entirely? On the other hand, how can we think and speak critically about real and persistent racial divisions if we allow racist language to silence us? Neither speech nor silence can perfectly preserve the illusion of a vantage point outside the moral failures of our culture. By choosing to use the word—to rub our noses in it, in fact—but ending with a self-mocking non-solution, Juanita makes us see that cosmetic changes to language only conceal racism, not eliminate it.

Adding to the moral ambiguity, "nigger" is a word traditionally used by whites to oppress blacks, but the homicide victim in this poem is a Latino immigrant who used the word in ignorance, and his assailants are African-American. Who is truly innocent here? The shooters, or men in their social world, might have felt they were resisting oppression by putting a positive spin on a word that the white majority used against them (the way some gays have reclaimed "queer"), but clearly the word still hurts them, no matter how tough they try to become by using it on each other. It's like keeping a loaded gun in your house: all it takes is one curious child to turn responsible self-defense into irresponsible risk.

Some interesting postmodern themes that arise
in this piece: "Bruno Was From Brazil" is a poem
about language that points to its own inadequacy,
yet cannot be silent. It's also about the disjunction
between signifier and signified. Repeat a word often
enough and it starts to sound strange, almost non-
sensical. Abstracted from its interpersonal context,
the word as word reveals itself to be empty, arbi-
trary. Yet this can lull us into a false sense of security,
because of course the interpersonal context is always
there, and the word in the real world always has
a history and an explosive charge. The author, the
speaker, is not in complete control of how the word
will be received. Is it "just a word"? Yes—and no.

The Gun as Ultimate Performance Poem

George Zimmerman killed Trayvon Martin, was acquitted for it, and has switched from security guard to painter, boxer, butcher, baker, and candle-stick-maker, whatever he wants. One round, point blank to the chest = a perfect exchange. A young life for his art. The Gun as art and culture.

The Gun as work of art. The Gun as art form and genre. The Gun makes history. The Gun as steel metaphor carrying the human urge to dominate and lay waste to an enemy or perceived threat. Guns as import and export. Hollywood's Gun, its cine-matic ordnance, is the United States' international calling card.

The Gun is oh-so-social, as it erases human inequality. Anyone can obtain one and point…shoot…kill. A bullet has no name, face, race, gender or class. The Gun is its microphone, the shooter but the stand for the microphone. The bullet is absolute, life-ending or life-changing, irreversible. The Gun is clean, leaving only smoke and powder in its wake. The Gun is the ultimate performance poem; the message in the poem is the bullet.

As much as I think I'm peaceable, I keep falling in with The Gun.

I moved back to my parents' house in East Oakland in 1990, in the middle of an intense drug war. My childhood home was a stone's throw from the notorious projects where heroin kingpin Felix Mitchell, as head of the 69 Mob, created an industry of drug trafficking as efficient for a decade as Henry Ford's assembly line. Felix the Cat's death in 1986 had left a fierce turf war in its wake. The nightly sequence I heard from my writing desk was spine-chilling: rapid machine gun fire, a car burning rubber as it screeched into the dark, silence for 10–12 minutes, then the ambulance siren. I never heard screams. Why were there no screams?

Without the noble purpose I conceived them to have when I was a young black militant, without art or revolutionary credo, these guns were unbearable microphones for a shattering community. Guns. Guns. Guns. I had liked guns.

Decades earlier, while a college junior, I joined the Black Panther Party in 1967 right when it split from a rival group of black cultural nationalists. Malcolm X's widow, Betty Shabazz, had come to San Francisco that February for a celebration of his life. One group called itself the Black Panther Party of Northern California, the other the Black Panther Party for Self-Defense; each agreed to meet her plane at the San Francisco airport with guns to protect her. One group showed up with loaded guns, the second came unloaded. The second group had no art, no ability to make history, no message. Though the second group was full of poets, writers, intellectuals and bright young minds, the first group prevailed and Huey Newton, Bobby Seale and Eldridge Cleaver joined the pantheon of holders of The Gun. The activists upstaged the artists/intellectuals. I had immense sympathy for the second group but pitied them (pitied their women more. How much subservience would soothe a wounded ego?).

The Gun was the shatterer of the boundary between the personal and the political. I liked guns. They were talismanic and palm-friendly. I liked being clandestine, carrying that .22 in my clutch purse when I went to work at the post office. The BPP labeled the intellectuals "paper panthers." This conflict between conscience and activism is not new. Stephen Spender, writing about the Oxford intellectuals said "detached intelligence" was a stance that a generation of anti-Fascists in the 1920s and 1930s rejected: "...personal values had to be sacrificed to the public cause. All that mattered was to defeat Fascism....choices had to be decided by the Marxist interpretation of history. Subjective motives did not count."

The split between the two groups of black militants shattered the viability of "detached intelligence" in the San Francisco Bay Area. The BPP cut through the pacifistic and rhetorical gestures and stance of the cultural nationalists with the pragmatism of the bullet. It resolved the issue of activism. How active should an activist be? Ready to die for the cause. The BPP resurrected the spirit of Nat Turner, Sojourner Truth and Harriet Tubman. The latter told her charges who wanted to return to the plantation once they'd gone underground: If you turn back, I'll shoot you.

The idea of carrying a loaded gun in May, 1967, into the legislative chambers of Sacramento, the dominion of Gov. Ronald Reagan, into the harsh deadly face of mid 20th century racist stolidity, rocked the world. Thirty black men, armed to the teeth and dressed in the signature beret and leather jackets, had the kind of impact that suicide bombers or serial killers have today. Scary.

The Gun is a revolt of the mind, an expulsion of hatred and thus a cleansing agent. Once it is fired, the act done, the two opposites are united forever, the killer and the killed written into history, memorialized or castigated.

To shun The Gun is to fear recklessness, to abhor chaos. Yet activists, oft called anarchistic, despise artists who don't overtly join them. Stanley Kunitz contends, "In a revolutionary period the activists are understandably disappointed in artists who do not overtly serve their movement. The Irish fighters for freedom despised (poet William Butler) Yeats for his failure to give them his unqualified support, not realizing that it was he who would immortalize their names and their cause..."

Bertolt Brecht said that a "conversation about trees is almost a crime because it involves keeping silent about so many misdeeds." The Black House in San Francisco flourished for a very short period (not as

long as Felix Mitchell's drug empire) in 1966 67.
I was there and no one was talking trees. Eldridge
Cleaver's book Soul on Ice was a bestseller and playwright Marvin X had plays on at SF State and in
community theaters. They formed The Black House
and opened it up for readings, political education
classes, poetry and dance performances, jazz and
lectures. In the Fillmore District, the Black House
was a seemingly perfect black counterpart for the
hippie and drug-oriented Haight-Ashbury. But its
split was not only political; in retrospect, its air had
a chauvinist aura. Women were often ornamental,
breeders not warriors, cooks and clericals, servers
not speakers, as if there to divert the heavy thinkers
from the heavy biz of the day—fighting the man.

Many cultural nationalists—LeRoi Jones (Amiri
Baraka), Don Lee (Haki Madhubuti), Sonia Sanchez—were poets, and poets were the shining lights
of the Black Arts Movement. Kunitz points out
that the writer works alone, unlike other workers,
and the poet is even more exceptional: "Among
writers the poet is freer than his brothers the novelist
and playwright, because his work, unlike theirs, is
practically worthless as a commodity. He is less subject than they to the pressure to modify the quality
of his work in order to produce an entertainment.
Nothing he can do will make his labor profitable.
He might as well yield to the beautiful temptation
to strive towards the purity of an absolute art."

Thus to look at the Black Arts Movement and its relation to the BPP renders a vision of the poets and dramatists standing in counterpoint. As student activists at SF State, the Black Student Union fought to bring Jones, Lee and Sanchez onto campus. We formed the Black Arts and Culture Troupe and toured community centers throughout the Bay Area with poetry, dance, and agit prop plays. We enacted ideas we were hearing on soapboxes about black power, black consciousness, and black beauty. We staged mock conflagrations like ones that were taking place in urban cities. We were empowering ourselves, our communities and getting academic credit. A natural progression was community activism. In 1967, my roommates and I joined the Black Panther Party which we found far more than a linguistic call to arms. It was a family, the place where you get together on holidays, tolerate the bigmouths, take care of each other, and keep it in the family, i.e. the secrets, the dirty laundry, the drunks, the incest, the beatings. Robyn Spencer, who interviewed former Black Panther women in the 1990s for her doctoral research, commented at our final interview that she was frustrated by our overall lack of forthrightness. I reminded her that there is no statute of limitations on murder, not that I knew of any such event.

However, the most important idea from that time, as I told another interviewer, was that we changed the language, the way black people thought and spoke, the way black people thought about how they were spoken about. A major assault on oppression is to assault it linguistically. The use of language and ritual had awed me in childhood where I loved communal gatherings, gospel fests, familial and religious celebrations. I'd worked since high school as a journalist but became disgusted with the field, its all-whiteness, narrow scope and predictability. When I started editing the BPP newspaper, I was embedded in the inner workings of the party, helping create the paper, typing, retyping, printing words and phrases like Off the pigs. Power to the people. All power to the people, Free Huey. My hands shocked me as they lettered and typed these words and the manifestos they formed. The BPP was appropriating the oppressor's language and using it to shatter oppression. That new use of language, in the BPP and in the Black Arts Movement, was as powerful as any gun and even more powerful because it aroused feeling and changed the terms of discourse between friends, enemies, lovers, generations and cultures. Being an agent of change meant I aroused deep feeling, affected discourse, found the powerful voices that I had heard in childhood, in church, in soul music, in the pulpit—within my own voice. Thus empowered, I began writing poetry, essays, and eventually moved on to drama and fiction. That was my start. Pre-Edward Said's Orientalism, two black males from the flatlands of Oakland, California, gave a voice to the oppressed using English in a wholly new way. Jean-Paul Sartre said the oppressed gain the use of the oppressor's language. In one instant, Off the Pig tossed back all the awful, dehumanizing, negative ways African-Americans had been characterized for two centuries. Baboons, coons, animals. To come up with this one phrase to describe abominable behavior, not physicality, was genius.

In Virgin Soul, my coming-of-age novel about that time, I handle The Gun often. The narrative would have lost its essence if I hadn't. At one point, protagonist Geniece shows her proper aunt the very first Black Panther Party newspaper. Her aunt recoils at the blood, guts and violence in Emory Douglas' artwork, with its copious use of the steely black metaphor. The Gun was an actual weapon carried and maintained by party members. It was Art. It was Metaphor. It was loaded with meaning and death.

Some would whitewash the civil rights movement and Dr. Martin Luther King Jr. into benign icons of a distant era, outsized statues or memories for annual celebration. Some would not see the movements for civil rights and black power nor the varied tactics of the NAACP, SCLC, SNCC, BPP, CORE, the Urban League, and the Nation of Islam as a spectrum of resistance against the racism that determined every facet of American life. The Black Panther Party for Self-Defense was the fist (The Gun, loaded, that is) of the kid (black people) who has been bullied (racism, oppression, legalized discrimination) long enough by the outsized bully on the block (US govt., US Constitution until 1865, opponents of Radical Reconstruction, Jim Crow, KKK, Bull Connor, etc.). Power concedes nothing without a demand, Frederick Douglass said. To demand is not to ask or beseech. That time when the streets were packed with citizens, students, protestors, workers, mothers against the war, unionists was not an acquiescent moment in this country's history. The numerous deaths are memorialized and well-documented. Did the moment peter out? Vanish into thin air? Not quite. The principles spread into society.

From the virgin soil of turbulence came the second wave of feminism and gay rights movements. The disabled emerged from seclusion and institutions to lobby for public access and accommodations. Senior citizens became Gray Panthers. Maria Gillan (a friend and fellow poet) became Maria Mazziotti Gillan, reclaiming her Italian-American roots and triggering the ethnic white literary movement at once. Bilingualism and Ebonics became recognized as essential curricula. Caucus as an intransitive verb meant your group agenda had to be strengthened privately and exhaustively to have maximum impact. Self-help, self-empowerment and self-enhancement became ideals because an entire society had watched the 97-pound weakling (black people) go from chump to champ. Black music, musicians and dancers became ambassadors-at-large to American society and the world. Duke Ellington and Count Basie had been there, done that. But the airwaves and new media amplified the beat, the dances, the Soul Train lines, the frizzy hair, the handshakes, the lingo (bro), none of which needed The Gun or its bullet because the BPP had handled that task. Our current heated debate about the n-word is permissible because of the BPP and Black Arts and Culture movement. Ishmael Reed, in grand old man fashion, came out with *Writin' Is Fightin': Thirty-Seven Years of Boxing on Paper* in 1988. The feat of aging gives one that Yeatsian right to write the story.

A few years ago, I woke up surrounded by Guns. Guns. Guns. My boss at the state arts council hosted me at her South Jersey home during my artist-in-residency. We'd had a falling out after her son had been killed in a hunting accident and she'd had three months of disarray and grief. Without money to meet my basic expenses and no checks coming in, my capacity for sympathy plunged. Angry words ensued. Eventually we made up and she invited me to her beautiful, starkly contemporary home nestled in the woods. We drank wine and talked late into the night; I looked through photo albums as she recounted how her grown children had been hunting when one fired the bullet that ricocheted and hit her son. He died in surgery. I went to sleep in the spare bedroom, too tired to take a good look around me. I woke up an hour later and turned on the light. The room was decorated with guns—handguns, rifles and guns with bayonets mounted in wooden and glass cases. I was sleeping in an ordnance. I tried to fall back asleep but couldn't dispel the images. In the moonlight I saw that the sheets on my bed had gun insignias all over them. For a moment, I thought I had gone crazy. Gun sheets? I had to do some serious calming down. The guns on the sheets and the walls were art, fashion and memorabilia.

I liked guns. I like mystery, intrigue, even devilment. My father was an avid reader of westerns, thrillers and detective novels. He had stacks of them next to his side of the bed. My mother had Bibles, loads of them, modern ones, illustrated ones, King James Version. As far as I could tell he never read from her side, and she never read any of his books…complete opposites married for 50 years. There was no gun. My mother said we couldn't even have sharp knives because tempers were too short in our household. I would like a society without The Gun. Too many short tempers in the world and this society. The BPP had a message that was received. As it deepened its focus in community service, the guns became less literal and more metaphoric and the party split into factions for and against The Gun. Internecine rivalries sprung up. I had moved far away spatially and spiritually.

I don't want gun control. I want police who are unarmed, peace officers. We can't have that unless we do away with guns. Maybe we can have parks where people play with guns the way we play with dinosaurs. That sounds like a shooting range. But it wouldn't be for target practice. It would be for fun. It wouldn't be a rehearsal for cruelty.

When Trayvon Martin was killed by The Gun, my heart ached. Trayvon was at risk because he didn't know how to cower, a posture that my generation destroyed. He didn't turn tail and run—although he might just have been shot in the back; he didn't yessuh back stepping. He fought George Zimmerman, toe-to-toe, and Zimmerman fired The Gun, at point blank range, because that was his creative moment. His high art. His historical moment. George Zimmerman united with his opposite Trayvon Martin forever. And the performances continue, in Aurora, Illinois, in Newtown, Connecticut, in schools and theaters and public spaces throughout the country. I liked guns. I hate The Gun.

All the Women in My Family Read Terry McMillan

I'm a black writer of literary fiction. My debut novel was published by Viking in 2013. I'm thrilled. But what a mission. The black chick lit phenomenon, heralded by Terry McMillan's *Waiting to Exhale* in 1992, exploded and led to new genres — urban fiction, street lit, gangsta fiction — which came to overshadow African-American literary fiction. The new genres have box office clout. A black female writer not writing chick lit has an uphill challenge. The proliferation of largely female black book clubs ensures that these novels are instructing a significant part of the black reading community.

It's ironic that these new genres have come to represent the whole of contemporary black literature. Langston Hughes honored the black vernacular and constructed "an entire literary tradition upon the actual spoken language of the black working and rural classes — the same vernacular language that the growing and mobile black middle classes considered embarrassing and demeaning."[1] The confining currently popular genres use selective pieces of the "actual spoken language" of a class of black people, which accounts in part for their colorful appeal. But the works often treat complexity and individuality elliptically. Yet they're popular. When I went to visit a male relative in the county jail and asked how he was faring, he replied that he had found a book by Omar Tyree and, by the way, jail wasn't all bad. Yet even McMillan has expressed disapproval of her literary progeny:

---

[1] Henry Louis Gates Jr., Langston Hughes, *Critical Perspectives Past and Present*. NY: Harper Perennial, 2000.

There are a lot of fine young new African-American writers out here. (But) I am not a fan of ghetto and urban lit.... I take seriously what they're writing about in terms of inner city life and all that. But I don't like the way that they tell their stories. It's not very redeeming. It seems that they glorify violence and hatred and self-hatred to me, to be very honest. And sex is gratuitous. I don't like the exploitation of black women's bodies on the covers of all the books that they use to sell them. And to me a lot of them are poorly written and unedited. And I think as black people we've struggled too long and too hard to try to be decent people and treat each other with a lot more respect and dignity. And these books just fall so short of it. It's almost as if they (the authors) don't even believe that we deserve it.[2]

Black literature, which I first devoured in the 60s/70s, included African-American speech in the urban zones, Adrienne Kennedy writing "The Funnyhouse of the Negro," the beat poetry of Bob Kaufman, the black nationalist ravings of Amiri Baraka, Ba'hai-influenced poetry of Robert Hayden, the chants of Sterling Brown, Gwendolyn Brooks' window on Chicago in poetry, and yes, Iceberg Slim's pimps. We were universal. There was no disconnecting Aimé Cesaire and Wole Soyinka's work and Claude Brown's *Manchild in the Promised Land*. We were part of a diaspora. We're still part of that; the whole of our literature isn't a trend.

---

[2] http://link.brightcove.com/services/player/bcpid57408845001?bctid=613867137001

In an ongoing attempt to counteract the trend, I
used my own writing and some unorthodox teaching to reach the very population that the publishing
industry has targeted. Being a community college
English instructor for nineteen years, I encountered
a young to middle-aged demographic that was urban,
literate, and decidedly not highbrow. I saw students
carrying and reading what some call "thug fiction."
This Oakland, California, open campus in the heart
of the city had roughly a third African-American,
a third Asian American, and a third "other"—that
includes whites and Native Americans. I couldn't
avoid their lives in literature.

I regularly used texts to broaden their perspective
(what teacher doesn't do that?). *Rosa Lee: a mother
and her family in urban America* by Leon Dash and
Makes Me Wanna Holler by Nathan McCall are as
gritty, provocative, urban and in-your-face as any
street fiction, yet they are greater teaching tools.
James MacBride's *Color of Water* and Frank McCourt's
Angela's Ashes strip poverty to its naked truth but
their strong literary elements illuminate the human
condition.

These then are my concerns. I don't want my tribe(s)
squashed into a tiny space. That's history. We don't
have to do it to ourselves. The detailing of the complexity and richness in human nature seems the
regular province of literature, more so than film or
television. I strive for that kind of contribution with
my writing.

Whatever Happened to Carolyn M. Rodgers?

There couldn't have been more than six people in the large auditorium of the Fruitvale Branch library in East Oakland, circa 1994. The poet, Carolyn M. Rodgers, read her work to the interested handful, her voice echoing in the empty auditorium. I was mortified at the turnout for this icon of the Black Arts Movement (BAM). Why weren't more poetry lovers there? Oakland Public Library newsletter and local papers had published ample notice of her appearance. While she wasn't a supernova like Sonia Sanchez or Angela Davis, she had published nine books of poetry. Blues poet and essayist Sterling Plumpp said of her work: "Between 1968 and 1978 I never believed that any female or male poet was any more crafted or gifted as Carolyn Rodgers. That is a fact."[1] Yet here she was, modestly reading her work to a handful of listeners. Was fame this fleeting?

[1] http://aalbc.com/authors/carolyn-rodgers.html

LEGENDARY SIXTIES POET

Rodgers was a seminal participant in the Black Arts Movement. In 1967, she founded Third World Press (TWP) with fellow poets Don L. Lee (later known as Haki Madhubuti) and Jewel C. Latimore (later known as Johari Amini). On a mimeo machine in a basement apartment on Chicago's South Side they started what became the country's largest independent black-owned press. Rodgers, a Chicago native born in 1940, earned her BA from Roosevelt University in 1965 and completed her M.A. in English from the University of Chicago in 1980. A central *padnuh* in the OBAC (Organization of Black American Culture) coterie, she prospered as it flourished. TWP published her first book, *Paper Soul* (1968). Hoyt Fuller, editor of *Negro Digest/Black World*, wrote the introduction.

Her second book, Songs of a Blackbird (1969), also from TWP, won the Poet Laureate Award of the Society of Midland Authors. In 1975, *how I got ovah: New and Selected Poems* was a finalist for a National Book Award.[2] Anchor Books published *The Heart as Ever Green: Poems* (1978). She established her own press, Eden Press, which issued *Finite Forms: Poems* (1985), *Morning Glory* (1989), and *We're Only Human* (1994). She also wrote plays, short fiction, and book reviews for the Chicago Daily News and a column for the Milwaukee Courier.[3]

Her emergence and dominant role in the Black Arts Movement would define her public life. Her rise in

---

[2] Cunningham, John. Encyclopedia Britannica. http://www.britannica.com/biography/Carolyn-M-Rodgers

[3] http://www.poetryfoundation.org/bio/carolyn-m-rodgers

the poetry world followed a familiar artistic pattern. Individuals are first recognized and nurtured at a school or in a movement; one later breaks with the in-group or it dissolves; the individual artist transcends or declines. Several such groups in the nineteen fifties and sixties influenced black artists and helped them get published. The Umbra Workshop in the 1960s, a Lower East Side artists collective, put Ishmael Reed, David Henderson, Steve Cannon and Calvin C. Hernton on the map. The beats gave LeRoi Jones (later known as Amiri Baraka) his lift-off; *The Journal of Black Dialogue* in San Francisco put Marvin X in orbit. The essential difference in Chicago was the presence of a woman mentor, Gwendolyn Brooks, a writer of Pulitzer Prize-stature. Rodgers didn't have to become Brooks' mistress, fuck buddy or wife to gain entry.

HER ILLUSTRIOUS FOREMOTHERS

Rodgers' poetic foremothers were Pulitzer Prize-winning poets. Gwendolyn Brooks and Margaret Walker were married and key figures in African-American literature in Chicago; their work, social activism and flirtation with the Communist Party surfaced in the 1930s-40s.[4] Gwendolyn Brooks, in 1968, embraced the "unruly roughness" of the new black poetry: "There's something very special happening in poetry today…among the young blacks. …I think after all of the activity… something will

---

[4] Washington, Mary Helen. *The Other Blacklist: The African American Literary and Cultural Left of the 1950s.* NY: Columbia University Press, 2014. See Chapter 14, "When Gwendolyn Brooks Wore Red," for a measured appraisal of Brooks' CP connection and "leftist race radicalism."

have been decided, and the poets will then have time to play more with their art."[5]

But this new paradigm of Blackness, though courageous, had its formalisms that at points wholly constituted its raison d'etre. Natural Hair was in, hotcombed, chemically-treated hair out. Fierceness replaced accommodation, hardness overpowered softness, and Godlessness supplanted God-fearing. Where blending had been a norm, being colorful was in, particularly for those who chose to call themselves Black v. Negro. It came down to empathy v. sympathy. If you were angered by the poet's voice, you perceived inside the boundaries. If you pitied the poet's voice, you were outside the boundaries.

Rodgers' poetry entered a world rife with conflict. The movement for civil rights, like the abolitionist movement 100+ years earlier, gained traction once the world took notice. Emancipation became foreseeable once Europeans, especially the British, understood the horror and treachery of slavery from abolitionists, slave narratives and ex-slaves travelling abroad. President John F. Kennedy's tepid response to the Emancipation Proclamation's 100th anniversary changed after pressure by civil rights activists; he approved the March on Washington.[6] The American workforce was changing as were TV, radio, pop records, magazines, fashion. Rhythm & Blues (R&B) was the persistent beat undercutting the click-and-slip of the pelvis in many popular dances

---

[5] *A Life of Gwendolyn Brooks*, George E. Kent. Lexington: University Press of Kentucky, 2009 (228).

[6] "The Kennedys were almost morbidly afraid of this march. They understood there'd been nothing like it," said Rep. Eleanor Holmes Norton, D-District of Columbia, who helped plan the march 50 years ago. http://www.cnn.com/2013/08/28/politics/march-on-washington-kennedy-jitters/index.html

of the time—the Boogaloo, Shimmy, Hully Gully, Hitch Hike, Popcorn, Jerk, Philly Dog, and Watusi. BAM poets—forerunners of hip hop, rap and slam poetry—were working the word as hard as they could, jerking, shimmying, boogalooing, popcorning, jerking and philly dogging in all the urban hot spots of the sixties. Rodgers' urban rhythm and insolence embodied the new black poetry and the urgency of the times. She was an avatar of the era.

A POIGNANT SET OF FISTICUFFS

In her work, Rodgers utilized language as a weapon to draw attention to larger social issues in an era that was an amalgam of social change. In "The Last M.F.," Rodgers defends her use of profanity by vowing to not use it, but to be, "as the new Black Womanhood suggests/a softer self…" Then, signaling a modern, intelligent, educated, outspoken, sistah for the ages won't be silenced, she writes "…I only call muthafuckas, muthafuckas/so no one should be insulted."[7] She's not only claiming her right to profanity, but her right to free speech, her right to be ornery, her right to not bow down. She embraced feminism and femininity on her own terms.

But as the BAM grew from rawness to maturation, paradigm shifts occurred in the religion of blackness, during and immediately after its establishment. Feminists and black lesbians contributed *womanist* to the dialogue. Offspring generations sampled R&B, reducing it to "the mix." After her flurry of writing fame in the sixties, Carolyn M. Rodgers became the phantom of the BAM, disappearing for

[7] http://www.english.illinois.edu/maps/poets/m_r/rodgers/about.htm

decades before resurfacing in her beloved Oakland, California, or native Chicago.

Many BAM poets changed up and even embraced other religions. A softened Sonia Sanchez joined the Nation of Islam for a spell; she was arguably the most militant yet lyrical female voice of the BAM. She commented recently on the softening of her work: "You must remember, in the time that we were writing, all the death and dying that happened and how we had discovered how much we'd been enslaved in this country…We came out hitting and slapping and alerting people to what had happened."[8]

Rodgers reconverted to Christianity, having set God aside. Did Rodgers' writing change after or during her reconversion? The change, the softening, would give strength to the notion that her return to God affected her poetry substantively. The vernacular changed. There is no swearing, no n-words, no sexually explicit wording in the new work she published at the start of the millennium. Not only does the language change, themes change. Revolution, rebellion, resistance — the themes of the BAM — flood her early work. Reconciliation, religious ecstasy, hope and eternity fill her later poems.

By 1994, living in Oakland, Rodgers stood in an East Oakland library reading old poems and recent ones in her ever-present head wrap of African cloth. The newer work relies on biblical references, and on salt as a metaphor. "In the Shadow of Turning" begins with "Throwing Salt/Teshuva: To Balance

---

[8] "Wear the Day Well: An Interview with Sonia Sanchez." *The Writer's Chronicle*. Feb. 2014:29.

the Scales." Teshuva is Hebrew for turning back to God, as with one who has left God:

> Since we use the
> good in our past
> to lead us to future good
> to remind us of what man is capable
> of, it seems
> right then that we
> should use the evil
> in our past also
> to remind us of what man
> is capable of.

That's her first stanza—proposition, theme, contention. The next line renders solution: "Salt is what/ it all becomes..." and later in the 26-line poem, a rueful observation: "The main event in life is something/We think we can plan, but can't..."

In middle age, Rodgers' mentor, Gwendolyn Brooks, became a different version of herself. She defied the pattern of female invisibility, leaving her husband (ultimately returning), becoming close to Don. L. Lee and leaving her New York publisher for Third World Press. She found Blackness with its unique themes and personalities at age 60. This radical change of direction was a phenomenon Rodgers would experience in middle age too; when confronted with illness, hypoglycemia and carbon monoxide poisoning, she used the same poignant fisticuffs and wordplay she'd socked at social problems:

when they told me I had it
they played it down. A low key
minor on a grand middle-aged piano
my life.
I must have had it right then.
I mean it must have had me in its tight fist...
I went around saying it silently and softly
to myself like
it was a new name someone had given me.
it was a sign of me to myself.
i am woman, negro, colored, then black.
Now
by pogly cemi a
a new name and because parts of me were missing
from a knockout bout with carbon monoxide
I walked around saying the word to myself
like it was a new name/trying to make myself
whole again.
even as I remained fragmented
from loss and pain.[9]

From the cradle up, grannies, aunties, mommas
teach what I call The Black Woman's National
Anthem: *you can do bad by yo-self.* Taking this
maxim to heart while embracing the open sexuality and unbridled militancy of the era, Rodgers,
Sonia Sanchez, et al, brought a new artistic voice
into the poetry community. With their parallels to
R&B, their uncommon voices crossed genres and
traduced boundaries, mixed slang, nostalgia, curse
words and sociological analysis, utilizing direct
speech and direct address, frank hope, frank distress,
sexual pleas for attention and raw revelation, sexual
intimacies, explicit language and confessionals that
evoked anger v. pity. The poems were manifestoes

---

[9] "A new Name." *ROOMS*, Vol. 4, No. 2. (Summer 1997).

of blatant and obscene phraseology that declared: we will not disavow one another. We are significant not insignificant. We stand in unity to avert disaster. The white woman can spit in her man's face (and 40 years later lean in). But we stand with you, brother. They addressed the abyss between black men and women by looking at it and acknowledging its presence as problematic issue in the community. This new work located the black community, despite dispersion due to migration, mobility and integration. Its black heart **was** the community unlike traditional poetry. It transgressed norms with obscene images of the black heart, the black pudenda, the black desire. Thomas Kuhn, the scientific philosopher who brought *paradigm shift* into the lexicon, said that intellectual courage is even rarer than physical courage. David Brooks said Kuhn realized that "an intellectually courageous person is willing to look at things that are surprisingly hard to look at."[10]

BEING MIDDLE AGED, TRANSITION, CONVERGENCE

By her 50s, when I met her in East Oakland, Carolyn Rodgers had survived carbon monoxide poisoning and fallen out of favor with black arts orthodoxy because of her espousal of Christianity. In "Salt: Prospective," Rodgers wrote about her concept of God: "all things may sometimes converge/God may be called that focal point/or some may call it light or truth or love..." Always mindful of divergence, her newer work sought togetherness.

---

[10] Brooks, David. "The Mental Virtues." NYT 8.28.14. http://www. nytimes.com/2014/08/29/opinion/david-brooks-the-mental-virtues. html?_r=0

"…at some point in any man or/woman's life, all/paths/roads/points/come together/for evil/or/ for good.[11]

What emerged was the philosopher poet exploring the human condition, nodding benevolently at contraries, no longer at war with the status quo.

Her lyric heart early on cried its independence in the midst of anxiety. In the much-anthologized "Poem for Some Black Women," she portrays the conflict between the necessity of hardness and the ideal of feminine softness:

> *…knowing the music of*
> *silence/hating it/hoarding it*
> *loving it/treasuring it,*
> *it often birthing our creativity*
> *we are lonely*
> *being soft and being hard*
> *supporting our selves, earning*
> *our own bread*
> *soft/hard/hard/soft*
> *knowing that need must not*
> *show…[12]*

Unlike Tyler Perry's Madea, who offers the world a head-snapping, celluloid Sapphire-in-perpetuity, Rodgers' poetic persona allowed women time to process anguish *and* bewilderment. She expressed the pain of being a black woman in a society that found black women as a whole at odds with its definition of femininity. She tackled the ideal of beauty, the quest for beauty, in "Some of Me Beauty":

---

[11] "Salt: Prospective." *ROOMS*. Vol. 4 No 4. Winter 1997.
[12] "Poem for Some Black Women." http://www.afropoets.net/carolyn-rodgers2.html

I went through my
Mean period
If you remember
I spit/out nails
Chewed tobacco on
The paper
And dipped some bad snuff… [13]

Tyler hides the pain in gruffness and sass, superficial responses that can deepen into bitterness if not resolved. Rodgers' early poetry embodied the snappy, cursing response that Madea has popularized. However, Rodgers opts for self-reflection, but gives it time. In "Some of Me Beauty," the pain changes two stanzas later:

…I woke up one/Morning
And looked at myself
And what I saw was
Carolyn
Not imani ma jua or soul
Sistah poetess of
The moment
I saw a woman. Human and
Black.

The BAM was perhaps the last time the noncommercial expression of black dialogue, the black aural expression, was representable. By the end of the black-is-beautiful phase, blackness was commodified. Integration meant not only school busing and affirmative action, but Blaxploitation movies, *Soul Train* as popular as *American Bandstand*, and the near-institutionalization of the black sidekick on TV and in movies. That would include

---

[13] Rodgers, Carolyn M. *How I Got Ovah: New and Selected Poems.* NY: Doubleday, 1976.

Huggy Bear on *Starsky and Hutch*, Alfonso Ribeiro as Alphonso Spears in *Silver Spoons*, Roger E. Mosley as TC Calvin in *Magnum P.I.* and Mr. T on *The A-Team*, to name a few. Diahann Carroll had the lead role as TV's "Julia" but was all gussied up and proper, her single parenthood transmogrified to a lunch-pail, antiseptic widowhood which conferred respectability. This was distinctly unlike her 1972 Oscar-nominated character in *Claudine* who had six kids out-of-wedlock.

Poets who became nationally prominent in the 70s and after included Rodgers' peers, Ntozake Shange, the late greats Lucille Clifton, Jayne Cortez and Wanda Coleman. All wrote poetry that was, by turn, fierce, wise and soft. The stance, the growl, the ferocity of the black arts movement poems had startled me as much as a Black orthodoxy felt restrictive. Were the poetic personas many black poets adopted professional necessity? Had they raged on the page and at the podium to aid and abet the revolutionary cause of the day? Were they forerunners for Tupac, Biggie, et al, who gangsterized their public image to match the simmering rage of being black and oppressed in America? Is being fierce a requisite part of being a *Black Public Person*? Though Rodgers has been called a metaphysical BAM poet, graciousness was not a part of the black arts orthodoxy.

But Rodgers turned to grace and graciousness after embracing Christianity. In her writing, she became a heretic and an ecumenicist, characteristically embracing opposites. When a radical friend trashed me for embracing Buddhism, Carolyn M. Rodgers

wrote "Ten Worlds" which melds Buddhism and
Christianity[14]:

> *my Buddhist friend*
> *tells me there are ten worlds.*
> *ten worlds. ten cesspools of sin?*
> *or ten sanctuaries and gateways to heaven(s).*
> *ten gardens of eden or*
> *ten paths to travel, to search through*
> *ten ways to laugh or cry and find or be*
> *found in....*
> *in the room of this house*
> *I am catholic and I drink the*
> *blood, eat the body of the lamb/god/man*
> *called Christ while my friend*
> *chants in another*
> *room of the house*
> *Nam-myoho-renge-kyo.*

This is some distance from the angst and loneliness of her sixties classic, "Poem for Some Black
Women," which expresses the dilemma of black
women[15]:

> *i am lonely,*
> *all the people i know*
> *i know too well*
> *there was comfort in that*
> *at first but now*
> *we know each other's miseries*
> > *too well*
> *we are*
> > *lonely women, who spend*
> *time waiting for*

---

[14] "Ten Worlds." *ROOMS.* Vol. 2 No 3. Fall 1995.
[15] "Poem for Some Black Women." http://www.afropoets.net/carolyn-
rodgers2.html

occasional flings....
we understand the world
problems
Black women's problems with
Black men
    but all
we really understand is
    lonely...

Although Rodgers did fly under the radar in middle-age, her work and Sonia Sanchez's poetry furnished several generations with new paradigms and language. Influenced by e.e.cummings' idiosyncratic grammar and punctuation, Rodgers and Sanchez, alongside Baraka, led the assault on tradition, transforming the Coleridge's "infinite I am" to "i am" and using repetition and alliteration to exploit cliché. When *news* becomes *noose*, meaning enlarges; calling the telephone cord "the witch cord" critiques AT&T and monopoly capitalism; calling Rodgers' mom a "religious-negro" who is "religiously girdled in/her god" is critique minus bitterness. "It is Deep (don't never forget the bridge that you crossed over on)" is one of her most quoted poems[16]; its classic ending led to the anthology *Sturdy Black Bridges: Visions of Black Women in Literature.*[17] Rodgers soldiered through the times, anthologized many times over, appearing in *Essence* and *O* magazines, speaking locally.

Often American poets and writers bravely face the theme of mortality toward the close of their lives like Raymond Carver, or on the battlefield, as Wilfred Owen's poems including "Dulce et Decorum

---

[16] http://www.english.illinois.edu/maps/poets/m_r/rodgers/online.htm
[17] Bell, Roseann P; Parker, Bettye J; Guy-Sheftall, Beverly. *Sturdy Black Bridges: Visions of Black Women in Literature.* NY: Anchor, 1979.

Est" highlighted World War I, or in facing terminal illness as Jane Kenyon's book, *Otherwise,* does. But, like Emily Dickinson, BAM poets always looked at death, farewell and departure, and created poetry of disengagement from a toxic and disparaging culture. In her life and work, my friend faced adversity with hopeful knowing. Rodgers knew the seriousness of her illness and talked from her poet's soul of mortality. We kept in contact until a few weeks before she died on April 2, 2010, in Chicago.

HER IMMEDIATE LEGACY

Carolyn M. Rodgers, Sonia Sanchez, Wanda Coleman, Jayne Cortez, Ntozake Shange and June Jordan opened the doors to the mainstream with frank, angry, unbridled, provocative, and, yes, sexually explicit, poetry. They changed the discourse of and about black women, of what had been repressed, surfacing only in bar rooms, smoky dives, or when uttered by raunchy female comics like Moms Mabley on the chitlin' circuit.[18] These educated and professional women poets of the 60s and 70s swept onto college campuses, bringing their publications, attitudes, funky demands and lifestyles. They toured and exposed students to their images and distinct voices, quickly becoming the foci of public radio and TV broadcasting. Throughout the 70s, a heyday for blacks on public TV, the BAM poets were all over Tony Brown's Journal, Soul!, WNET New York, For You Black Woman (hosted

---

[18]"During the years before the Civil Rights movement got underway, segregated American cities helped give birth to a touring circuit that provided employment for hundreds of black musicians and eventually brought about the birth of rock 'n' roll." http://www.npr.org/2011/12/20/140596530/before-rock-n-roll-the-chitlin-circuit-performed

by Freda Payne), Say Brother, WGBH Boston, Harambee, NYC, Like It Is, WABC-NYC, WTOP-D.C., to name a few.[19]

Shange took her choreopoem, "For Colored Girls Who Have Considered Suicide When the Rainbow is Enuf," from northern California bars to The Public Theater in New York, on to Broadway and book publication. Even though her play polarized some black men and women, it brought into public view the stark, often tragic dissonance between black female romantic expectation and its realization. Shange's dance and poetry employed a generation of women actors and dancers who vocalized the frustrations of being black, female and dispossessed. They went on to mentor the next generation which walked through the doors of affirmative action with sexiness and independence.

Without the black women poets of the sixties breaking through, there would be no Beyoncé on the cover of TIME in her booty pants, no Audra MacDonald being the most celebrated Broadway actress ever, no Mae Jemison astronaut falling gracefully in space, no Oprah and Gayle/paradigmatic girlfriends influencing cultural politics, no Sistah Souljah being called out by a faux-black Bill Clinton. Nor would Salt-N-Pepa, Cheryl James, Sandra Denton and Deidra Roper ("Salt," "Pepa," and "DJ Spinderella"), have had the poetic license to talk provocatively and gyrate their pelvises exponentially harder than Elvis. Salt-N-Pepa became the first female rap group with huge hits in the US and United Kingdom. Unlike the blues singers and

[19]For a comprehensive list of black public broadcasting TV programs, see http://www.thirteen.org/broadcastingwhileblack/uncategorized/list-of-black-produced-tv-shows-nationwide-from-1968-on/

black strippers ("shake dancers") who had gotten
down and dirty behind closed doors in the repres-
sive decades before the sixties, Salt-N-Pepa strutted
their sexuality on an international stage, a form of
sexual politic neither marginalized nor hidden from
public view.

Whatever happened to Carolyn M. Rodgers? She
transcended herself and her early public persona.
But her initial work lit up the literary scene and
fired up the public voice of the black woman.

APPENDIX I

Some letters from Carolyn M. Rodgers to Judy Juanita.

Carolyn and I began communicating through snail and e-mail in 2004; we continued corresponding until two weeks before she died in 2010. After the first salutation (Hi Judy), I've chosen to omit the others but include dates.

Nov. 9, 2004

Hi Judy,

I am just hanging on here. In Chicago, people are pretty sobered after the election and blame is going everywhere. I had to have oral surgery Saturday and I have stitches in my mouth, so I'm not debating anybody about anything much!

I went to my second conference though yesterday, for women who want to start their own business. It was held at the Hyatt Hotel here and I had been planning to attend for months; I wasn't about to stay home because of my mouth. I'm so glad I went. It was all about woman power! Women of every race, creed, and color, (to borrow a cliché) were there, and we were all trying to break the glass ceiling, among other things. I wouldn't have missed it for the world.

I would like to learn how to create a web site. I am hoping that when I do go back to teach it will only be for a short time. But who knows? I might get a real good (book) deal, anyway, as we settle in, for what lies ahead. Thanks for putting me on your mailing list. There is so much good head food that you send me. Sometimes, I am awed by people's capacity to still articulate in extremely erudite, yet down-to-earth fashion, the challenges that we face today. Everybody here was overjoyed that Barack Obama won over Alan Keyes. I'm guessing that you know who those two are.

The Black community here though is still quite stunned and Jesse Jackson held a historic meeting with Minister Farrakhan and they talked about what our new challenges are. People were invited to comment and it was all very good and helpful.

So, life goes on....Keep the faith! Chant some good things for me and I will affirm good things for you!!!

luv Ya! Carolyn

Mar 3, 2005

I don't guess I ever told you about the time I was asked to speak at SIU (Southern Illinois University). It's a big campus here in Illinois, and carries a lot of prestige here in the state. The black students had just been given a new campus house for their functions and they had named it after Gwendolyn Brooks. I was very excited about going there to read my poetry. The letter stated that I would receive $450, plus traveling and eating expenses. Not bad. So I went.

Not one single student showed up for the reading! Not one! The first and last time it ever happened to me! They made some lame excuse and said that students were probably busy studying for finals. I was given my check (glory, glory) and I took my wounded pride home. Several days later, I received a letter saying that they were sorry that I had not been paid (!) and they sent me a second check. An obvious mistake! It doesn't get much better than that. It doesn't get much worse than that; by this I mean no one showing up!

Things will get better, I'm sure. You learn from it all. Hopefully, one day we will look back and laugh at it all! Hang tough!

Luv Ya! Carolyn

Feb 19, 2005

.... I found one of my old essays where I was using the f-word all over the place! Now I know what they liked about me. I had forgotten me. I was almost completely irreverent at times, and might I say with gusto and flair! I couldn't believe who I was. It was real food for thought. No wonder they look at me the way they do now! I still believe that half the battle though in getting published is who you know. I was very lucky to be in Chicago with Gwendolyn Brooks and many famous literary people came to sit at her table and I met them. I believe though that you have to keep on putting yourself out there. That's what I have to do; otherwise I am an interesting artifact. Or as I told some of my students, I'm history, literally.

Keep the faith. I love the sunshine and laughter you keep sending. My days are getting brighter. Definitely! Hope yours are too.

Feb 12, 2005

I was most appreciative of the interview that you sent me. Ossie Davis & Ruby Dee have been friends of mine for a long time! Years ago, Ruby came to Chicago to do a reading and she was using one of my poems. She asked if anyone knew how to get in contact with me. She thought I might like to see the performance. Hence, the beginning of a long friendship. I was in Walgreen's buying some stuff and the Black salesgirl, (a young girl) told me (about Ossie Davis' passing). I knew then that he had indeed left an indelible and lasting mark. She was barely twenty and she was saddened by his passing. I was overwhelmed, right there in the store. But in my life, that's how things are right now. We all have this curtain call.

And I'm busy living and trying to love my life as much as possible, hoping I get it all together and have plenty of time to do it!

I want to teach five classes in one class. Happy Valentine's Day!

Jan 5, 2005

One of my friends who lives in Oakland has for the last twenty-five years come home to Chicago for the holidays. I got a visual tour of my beloved Oakland, through her eyesight! More than ever, I'm pledged to get back there! I can hardly wait. I have no illusions about some of the problems. They were there when I was last there. But what has that got to do with loving the place?

Sept 27, 2004

I just got your piece from E.L. Doctorow. It sorta blew me away! I just pulled it down/printed it out, and it made me want to write my own poem about the war and everything. I haven't finished reading the piece yet, but I wanted to respond quickly. Sometimes, it takes days for me to get to my e-mail. I don't do anything except work since I quit work! I can't believe I have even less time, but it almost seems that way.

I miss my job. And more than anything else, I miss getting paid every two weeks, even if it was almost slave labor. But the weather in Chicago in autumn is unbelievably beautiful, so I'm enjoying that. Especially, since it definitely isn't going to last. Maya Angelou was in our city tonight for a book signing. More to come. I'm just a rambling rose right now.

April 5, 2005

I am finally making some headway. And I don't mind telling you that your emails give me much motivation. I'm not just out here, "all by myself" trying to make it work/or happen! In the last two months I have bought 3 different pieces of software to do chapbooks with. Finally, it looks like one of them is going to work! It is actually viable, and I have been able to begin a decent dummy again. Glory, glory! smile.

You are the playwright that I still want to be! I can't get to my plays yet at all. Too much going on around me..... I don't know anymore how I had time to work! I will have to make drastic changes for this upcoming job in the fall. It's a seminar on older Black writers, like G. Brooks, Margaret Walker, Langston Hughes, Richard Wright, et al....So, life goes on.

May 19, 2005

I just had to share the good news. After not receiving any royalty statements from Doubleday for the last three years, I figured the little glory ride was over! But lo and behold (!), what was in my P.O. box but a statement with a small check, after three long years. It made my day, possibly my year! smile. Now all I need is a little more macho to approach them about a book contract. I've queried them about that for the last five years, at least, and never even received an answer back. Well, too bad for them...

Jan 17, 2008

I have been corresponding for at least two years, probably more, with a PH.D. Black history professor at _____. He was writing a book, his third or fourth to be published, and he wrote me about using some of my work and that's how it started. Through my illness and madness and everything, he was right there. Well, I hadn't heard from him for a few weeks, and I'd sent him a Christmas card. I thought it odd that I hadn't heard from him but he was the Chairperson of the African-American/Black Studies Department there, so he was very very busy, at times. Well last week I got the card back. A note was scribbled on it, which simply said "sorry, deceased." I almost fainted. What? He was 62 years old and happily planning his retirement!!! I couldn't believe it!

So I called the school and his secretary told me that he had slipped and he fell and fractured his skull in the parking lot when he was keeping a doctor's appointment! And that was it... I am a changed woman. Life keeps making me change, just when I think I can handle it all or it's all okay or this or that, something happens. He had been teaching for 34 years and was looking forward to retiring. He's written 7 books and had 3 more coming. It scared me. It intimidated me....And to make matters worse here, the sun has all but abandoned Chicago. For days on end we are overcast. It is gloomy, and dark, many days, one right after the other. We all have SAD, Seasonal Affective Disorder, and today it is just almost 3 o'clock and it's almost dark. It's too much! For this cause, in 1986, I left Chicago and first moved to Oakland.

What's happening on your end of the world? We're holding fort here.

(Like so many, Carolyn was overjoyed at Barack Obama's Presidential win.)

Nov 10, 2008

How lucky I am! I was standing on the corner (Friday) where I live, which is directly across the street from where Obama goes to work out, when I look up and what do I see but a string of about 20 black, long limos, with Obama and God knows how many secret service men, and University of Chicago students of every race, creed, and color running along the street, wildly, holding up their cell phones with the cameras, yelling "I got one." I just stood there frozen in time, finally able to lift my arm and wave at this wonderful man in this long stream of sleek shiny black cars, policemen, in front and behind. I wish I had grandchildren to tell it to! It made my day, you know, and everybody else's, waiting for the bus!

Feb 25, 2010

Finally I'm back to life again, back to reality as the song says. Last night I read poetry with Sonia Sanchez and Angela Jackson and the day before I was so sick and had been so sick for weeks, I could hardly do a thing. They put some happy gas in my IV, gave me 2 pints/units of blood and I was good to go. I think I'm just coming down. Only to hear from Sonia at the poetry reading that Lucille Clifton made her commitment/ or transition as some people call it.

Girl, things are happening. I know everybody was watching me these last few weeks and quiet as it's kept, I been watching some of them. I am trying to enjoy life as much as I can. I'm taking it easy. I'm laughing, and I think this is the way. I have to watch my blood pressure now. My feet are so swollen I cannot even get them in my boots. My legs are swollen too. I have to take diuretics and then run run run to guess where. I just laugh it off. What else is new?

Feb 26, 2010

Each day I am more impressed about youth and age. I am so glad I have been allowed to grow "old" shall we say? I love being an elder and I love the children. They are precious and I see me and others I know and don't know going and coming. You know what I mean? Somedays I want to say, this one or that one is back on earth again???? Let's hang in there. I feel so good today if only in my spirit and soul, well not only but mostly. I fully plan to make it back to Oakland one day soon. It is one of my goals for 2010 or 2011, hopefully the former! I was telling Sonia S., I would love to host a gathering of Black women writers from the '60's and maybe not only Black... What do you think? I'm seriously sighting places trying to figure out how to pull it off. If you have any ideas about it, cue me in. Keep the faith.

Obviously, I live in a very posh neighborhood. Usually, I don't think much about it, because it is University turf and it's my SISTER's money, obviously not mine! (smile).

(Obama's) neighborhood office is in the building on the sixteenth floor, and we look over at it from our living room. I calm myself, or I am constantly hyperventilating! (smile).

What a world. What a life. Can't help lovin' it.

De Facto Feminism

A comic in the Bay Area used to open every set
reciting the outrageous black names he'd heard
while teaching at Berkeley High School — cheap
trick, cheap laughs. I empathized with those youth
carving out their destinies with their hybridized
names, echoing distant Africa, Frenchification, and
urban preciousness. The 1960s — my youth — were
the last period when blacks on a large scale changed
their names from Anglo-Saxon — *what was your
slave name?* — to African-influenced surnames and
first names. To hear another generation in search
of identity mocked, over and over, infuriated me.
When I hear those names and know they've become
a national punch line, I feel insulted, branded,

*Ednitra Quintricious Bunquisha Shaniqua
Jamarius Larquell Tasheanna Krisshaya
Trayvon Shivon Adneeshia*

further marginalized, objectified and made invisible
again. And it's not as if these names don't perplex
black people too. As I heard someone say, "You just
taking all these strange names to confuse white
people." Dave Chappelle defended the phenomenon in a San Francisco comedy club to a crowd of
coders, Gen X-ers and millennials. Chappelle said
these names are an act of rebellion to racism by the
women naming their babies. I got him. The names
function as comeback, rebuttal to little black Sambo,
to black memorabilia going for exorbitant prices,
for outsized clay lips painted bright red, to white
college kids having black days with watermelon and
ersatz food stamps. With his gee whiz/I'm a stoner,
almost-shuffling demeanor, Chappelle nailed it.

These children, amid the hostility, superiority and racism of teachers, media makers and prospective and current employers, form part of what I call de facto feminism.

De facto feminism is like de facto segregation, which remains the way our nation is organized. De facto segregation is the practical reality of separation of members of different races, not by law (de jure), government action or statute, but in practice by various social and economic factors. Blacks live in Bed-Stuy and East St. Louis, Mexicanos in the barrio, whites in suburbia and gated communities.

Place the synonyms for de facto in front of feminist: absolutely, actual, actually, as a matter of fact, authentic, bona fide, certain, demonstrable, existent, existing in fact, factual, genuine, in reality, positively, real, substantive, true, unquestionable, valid, veritable. What do you have? Black women. En masse.

20th c. Feminism: defensive, lean-in elite, scarce, historical, white-ish, precious, theoretical, lawful, contempt for men but not their $$$

De facto feminism: *offensive, classless, proliferative, ahistorical, black and then some, inside/outside the law, do-you with/without men*

BLACK WOMEN = DE FACTO FEMINISTS

Black women are de facto feminists, including the young parents naming their babies Daquan, Tanisha, Aiyana, Tarika, Ramarley, Kendrec, only to be slaughtered by police alongside the Anglo-Saxon named children, the Michaels, the Oscars. Black women can't fake feminism, hide it or disappear into marriage. They don't do it for a season, dodge it, or veil it in a career. They can't be faux feminists insulated by class privilege. De facto feminists stand between peace and war every day in Detroit, Oakland, Harlem, Miami, Chicago, St. Louis, Dallas, the White House, The View, Philly, Baltimore, LA—the Gaza Strips of the US—without glorification, often vilified as big fat mama... hefty cinch sack... wide-assed tub of lard...Ubangi bitch...monkey face...Aunt Jemima...Sapphire. They straddle fences, take flak from both sides, get called accomodationists, build straw bridges and cross them undaunted, raise their villages, and for that they have developed a following. Like ducklings (flocks?), not always acknowledged nor conscious, devotees of black women nevertheless have developed.

"AIN'T I A WOMAN?"
—Sojourner Truth, 1851,
Women's Convention, Akron, Ohio

Isabella Baumfree, born a slave in 1797 in upstate New York, was auctioned off at ten for $100 alongside a herd of sheep, but freed herself by escaping in 1829, going through excruciating hardships and court battles, some of which she won, and becoming a renowned speaker and agitator for women's and black rights. She changed her own name to Sojourner Truth in 1843. Her "Ain't I a Woman" speech was given impromptu, no speechwriter or publicist holding her hand, although, because of her illiteracy, helpers wrote down her words. Thank goodness.

De facto feminists are modern day Sojourners, who can't always operate openly. In many housing projects throughout this land, the Candy Lady reigns.

An entrepreneur, she shops at Costco, Big Lots and Dollar Tree—alongside her East Indian, Chinese and Korean counterparts—for packaged groceries, toiletries, candy, soda, and liquor in bulk. She goes back to the projects, carries the inventory upstairs and sells it to her neighbors. On the straight and narrow, she purchases goods at retail, pays taxes at the register. On the precipice, she operates minus a license, doesn't report profits on federal and state taxes, sells 24/7/365, trades cigarettes and liquor to adults and minors for barter, cash, food stamps and contraband. Ain't she a feminist?

A short list of off-the-books occupations practiced relentlessly by urban and working poor includes kitchen beautician, childcare worker, housekeeper, tutor, elder companion, pet sitter, house sitter, tax-return preparer, Candy Lady, domestic, errand runner, driver, caterer/cook, caregiver, flea marketer, dressmaker, prostitute, drug dealer, drug packager, street vendor, software and movie pirate, taxicab hack, shoplifter, astrologer, psychic, tarot reader, gardener, lawn mower, party DJ, typist and writer. There are other names for them. Outlaws. Outliers. Rebels. Revolutionaries. Citizens. Patriots. Tax cheats. Black markets flourish in times of war, like we're in now. I've done my share; I know whereof I speak. How many of these are performed habitually by women? Ain't they a feminist?

"The Internal Revenue Service esti
mated that the losses from unreported
wages have grown from about $385 bil-
lion in 2006 to about $500 billion last
year. State governments lose another
$50 billion to the overall underground
economy. That means the people who
play by the rules are getting a raw deal."[1]

THE LAND OF SINGLE PARENTING

A number of black women hit their mid to late-
twenties, look around and see no Prince Charming.
They conclude he's not on his way. They decide to
have a baby and sally forth into the Land of Single
Parenting. They have the village on their side, the
army of mama, grandmamma, auntie, uncle, cousin,
nephew, niece, play cousin who have never listened
to a hoary Dr. Laura tell her distressed listeners to
put their unborn up for adoption.[2] We don't do
that, I've shouted her voice down on my car radio.
Baby mommas well before the trend. And ain't
they feminists?

My mother, Marguerite Juanita Hart, put up with
unchecked racism, sexism and, lastly, ageism her
entire working life as a printer/typographer for
federal and state governments. She trained young
whites who were as often as not promoted over
her; they then turned around and lorded it over her.
I took her middle name as my last to honor this
unrecognized and valiant part of her. One good
effect in her long bout with Alzheimer's was the
loss of those bitter workplace memories. When I

---

[1] Money Morning, http://moneymorning.com/2013/04/29/what
americas-2-trillion-underground-economy-says-about-jobs/
[2] http://www.drlaurablog.com/category/adoption/)

divorced and used her middle name as my surname, friends in New York feared people might mistake me for a Puerto Rican. My dad said my maiden name was good enough to use again. My in-laws, the T____s, sent me gold pins initialed J. T. My mother said, "After all black people have done to be legitimate and get married, why would you want to walk around with two first names?" My important post-divorce lesson: satisfying me might mean displeasing all others. Nevertheless, mother pleasing, daughter displeasing—ain't we a feminist?

TRYING TO MAKE A DOLLAR OUT OF 15 CENTS

A whole class of workers constitutes women who braid hair, part of the underground economy in the black community. Overwhelmingly black and youthful, they work from home, a cadre of postmodern kitchen beauticians who make a way out of no way to raise children, make money, be stylish and create community. I've paid increasing amounts for their services, to *get my hair did*, because they do a good job. They often combine this income with public aid or Section-8 subsidies to make it in this society.

For the past twelve years, Sakeena has "allowed" her first child's father to live in her Section-8 apartment with her and her other two kids, sort of a Section-8 largesse. Women with children and Section 8 act as quasi-landlords with their off-the-books tenants. In New Jersey, I lived in a six-unit building with several foxy single mothers who attracted and "housed" members of the New York Giants football team during the season. Over the decade I lived there, a rotating cast of ballers paid their ladies' way and no small amount of dentistry for said ladies and their offspring, clothes and food (and thrilled my son and his Pop Warner teammates).

This blur of legality, morality and practicality at the heart of de facto activity has been a feature of African-American life since the first Africans arrived on these shores — and a part of immigrant life. Making it in America means going from the margin to the mainstream, not so easy in one generation. The stigma that black people carry as pigment forces them to be what others would term illegal, immoral but not impractical. The dividing line between feminism and black independence is necessity.

This blur of legality, morality and practicality at the heart of de facto activity has been a feature of African-American life since the first Africans arrived on these shores.

Valencia has never been to jail, not once, though she's run numerous scams. One perennial fleece involves the US mail, 100 recipes for five bucks, and a P.O. Box. She has yet to send out one recipe but collects those green dollars religiously. All the while, she made sure her exceptionally bright girls got top educations, terminal degrees, and became respectable professionals. Is this Mario Puzo's country or what? Valencia started her "career" early. She'd spoon all the fruit from the Jell-O before her siblings got to it, the same siblings who have college degrees and professional jobs, unlike Valencia, she who learned to be cunning but raised daughters to live straight and narrow. Feminist, eh?

Shelley at nineteen had a brick shithouse figure, a five-octave voice and sweetness to spare. She also had a disinclination to sell her body for a recording contract. She languished in the bush leagues of jazz vocalists for years before the call came. She answered, left for Los Angeles, but not everyone has the stomach to sleep their way to the top, as Elton John's "Goodbye Yellow Brick Road" makes clear. Shelley eventually had success, not as fast or as spectacular as she might have had in LA, but she didn't sell out. Maybe her mother told her, as Marguerite told me: "Never sell your soul. Your body. Or your country." Oh my, ain't she a feminist?

This making a way out of no way, nurturing those who've been forgotten or discarded, are hallmarks of a de facto feminist.

Oral Lee Brown grew up one of 12 children in the Mississippi Delta, moving to Oakland at 18. She went to school at night and worked in insurance before becoming a realtor. When she promised a class of first graders deep in the flatlands that, if they kept a "C" average through high school she would send them to college, she had no idea where the funds were. But she had been moved to this great vow by the story of one girl who couldn't make it to school because of a troubled home life. Eighteen children went all the way through college, two were killed in gang activities and two got into drugs. Ms. Brown's foundation continues to incentivize hundreds of at-risk Oakland students. This making a way out of no way, nurturing those who've been forgotten or discarded are hallmarks of a de facto feminist.[3]

---

[3] http://www.womensconference.org/oral-lee-brown/

ROXANE, CAN WE TALK?

Even a fresh voice like Roxane Gay becomes an apologist if she only deigns to be complicit in the last century's scheme of things. When she says misperceptions about Haiti as dangerous and poverty-stricken make it hard to write about, I like that. When she says there are both falsities and truths behind the Haitian stereotypes, I warm to her. Giving blow jobs gratis — part of Gay's bad fem history — might not be prescriptive for women who need the money to make the rent. A new wave of feminists instead might envision women of color setting policy and leading, being arbiters versus being left behind. The 21st century may define for itself who and what a feminist is. New contradictions, caused by more intense oppression, immigration and higher barriers to workplace freedom and social equality, will lead to dystopia or revolt.[4]

Arwilda, an army wife, living off-base in Seattle in 1954, called the local police when her husband, the only black staff sergeant on base, ordered her to wash the supper dishes. His manner frightened her. The police, so her daughter told me, laughed at Arwilda and told her husband he was fully within his rights, i.e. women wash dishes, men order them to. Weren't she a feminist in the 1950s with her fourth-grade education, Ph.D. from the school of hard knocks, speaking truth to power — husband power, military power, and police power — in her own kitchen?

---

[4] http://www.chicagomag.com/Chicago-Magazine/May-2014/Roxane-Gay/

All of them, Arwilda, Sakeena, Valencia, Shelley and my mother, are far more feminist than the broadcasters/weathercasters who've memorized feminist principles and theory from prep school through the Ivy League. They learn all this to bare cleavage and toned limbs to sexist news directors and producers who trade tapes of them for private showing (one of the dirty little secrets of the broadcast industry). Are they feminists? It's hard to answer in the affirmative when one mistakes being a frontispiece for being on the front lines. Ah, it works in reverse—what applies to the goose applies to the gander. Titles and categories devolve into discrete units that obliterate and turn people into "others" without their consent. Being a de facto feminist means your body, voice, fists, sense of indignation has to fight at the barricades, whether you feel like it or not.

I adjudicate otherness at the barricades daily, e.g. when I called the police because my neighbor was beating his girlfriend. Having been a Black Panther in the 60s wasn't even a consideration when I dialed 911. When male students try to intimidate me into changing a grade, I tell them that female students rarely use this approach. When male drivers expect me to give up my right-of-way, I often don't. In little and big ways, women are challenged to give in or give up. To stand up can be isolating, frightening, seen as threatening, and finally lethal. When I used an IUD for a year and a half, I routinely saw blood clots, big as mice, in my bathwater. When I later met someone who casually said she'd had fifteen abortions, I was aghast. How could she? I've continued to meet younger women who have, indeed, used Planned Parenthood as a post conception disposal chute. I can set aside the argument that Margaret Sanger founded the organization as eugenics/genocidal scheme.[5] Yet I condemned the doers — young desperate women, their partners and Planned Parenthood facilitators — until I recalled those fuchsia globs, week after week, floating around my body. I hadn't wanted another baby inside an unhappy union. I had been financially strapped. I hadn't dared to have another baby when I was overwhelmed with the care of one. For years I chalked up my interminable birth control hunt (pills, creams, diaphragm, IUD, herbs like gentian root) to the perils of modern medicine. We're all guinea pigs, I'd shout to the heavens, as one or another method failed or displeased me or a partner. But these women ending pregnancy in this stumblebum way splintered my rationalizations and self-defense. Had I been so different? Those clots represented my fertility, if not literally, then figuratively. Some women freeze their eggs. Others hatch or dispose of them. Some let nature take its course. Some stubborn ones of us will the unseen out of our systems. And some let modern medicine be the overseer. How can I judge the woman with fifteen abortions until I can count how many I've had?

"I sell the shadow to support the substance"
— Sojourner Truth

First and second-wave suffragettes are due full credit for the tremendous advances in women's liberation. Surely Sojourner Truth devoted her life to the struggle for freedom and was enabled by women and abolitionists struggling at the same moment in history. She sold pictures of herself, not

[5] http://www.nytimes.com/2010/02/27/us/27race.html?sq=to%20 court%20blacks,%20foes%20

in chains or with scars of enslavement on her back as other ex-slaves were doing, but in traditional portrait pose, knitting, fully clothed, strong. She wrote herstory. In protest movements, as in wars, the people on the bottom don't write history. The literate and highly literate do that, historians, writers and editors, mostly male. Movements occur. Records are kept. Schools of thought develop. Championing and advancing the cause of the downtrodden, e.g. women under the yoke of sexism and enslaved Africans, has its noble side; yet even the illustrious can be faulted with taking undue credit or showboating. The tight hats of pride, self-congratulation and exclusion in the feminist movement were worn in the abolitionist movement too.

Many abolitionists acted on behalf of the enslaved who lacked agency. Antebellum diarists recorded the thoughts and responses of those forbidden family, community, literacy, citizenship and freedom of movement. Historian John Blassingame's landmark book *Slave Testimony*[6] instigated what Henry Louis Gates, Jr. called "the revolution in historiography." Letters written by slaves and former slaves date from 1800[7]. That's 177 years (!!!) before Blassingame began the process of setting the record straight—a record he found impressive but marred by disregard and questionable ethics ("whites edited narratives because their interest in slavery had been aroused by sensational trials involving kidnapped or fugitive blacks").

[6] LSU Press, 1977.

[7] Carter G. Woodson discusses these letters in *The Mind of the Negro as Reflected in Letters Written During the Crisis, 1800-1860*. The Association for the Study of Negro Life and History, Inc., Washington, DC, 1926 edition: http://store.doverpublications

Will it take 200 years for respect to come to the de facto feminists sitting on the bottom, squeezed into pink collar ghettoes and brown security guard uniforms, lined up at the minimum wage margins of this world? I hope not. *The Washington Post* reported, in 2014, alarming and shocking news about black women: maternal death rate is triple that of white women, that five of us die of breast cancer every day because we lack access to life-care; that our hypertension rate tops every other demographic group; that when we age, our over-65 income is the lowest of any group, and poverty at that vulnerable point is startlingly higher than others; and because we marry less and divorce more, even our Social Security spousal or widow benefits are markedly lower. These "stubborn differences (that) persist across both race and gender in America," this report asserts, hit black women the hardest.[8]

On the heels of this alarm is a story from *The Atlantic* about black America. "Black America resembles countries like Brazil, China, and Russia — emerging powers that are struggling with stark economic inequality." If the nation/state of black Americans is in woeful condition, black women within are double done for.[9]

Maybe it's inevitable that privileged participants in a class struggle end up more privileged as the underprivileged inch up to make way for a new group to layer the bottom — not everyone can do the Ché Guevara tango from doctor's son to guerrilla to

[8] http://www.washingtonpost.com/r/2010-2019/
WashingtonPost/2014/03/27/National-Politics/Stories/2FinalBlack-
WomenintheUS2014.pdf
[9] http://www.theatlantic.com/national/archive/2014/10/what-if-black-
america-were-a-country/380953/

martyr. Ubiquitous de facto feminists are walking, talking political education classes who teach persistence when things don't work out, when no one comes to help or when facing death. They might even be goddesses or shamans, god forbid.

CHOICES, SEXUAL AND OTHERWISE

The increased acceptance and occurrences of lesbianism, careerism, intermarriage, abstention from sexual relations or marriage and becoming an expatriate (i.e. leaving black America behind and, of course, encountering other problems) have yielded a generation of women with alternative choices and lifestyles without the disgrace, ignominy, loneliness or mortification that their mothers or women of previous generations met. Hands-on celibacy became my unspoken choice for years until herpes, AIDS and the papillomavirus made celibacy quasi-mandatory for the rest of society. Feminist, no?

After emancipation, as Angela Davis details in *Blues Legacies and Black Feminism*, African-American men and women were flat broke but free to create the blues.[10] That new American art was an "aesthetic evidence of new psychosexual realities within the black population….no less impoverished" because they hadn't money or means. What changed was their freedom to choose sexual partners. Davis asserts, "Sexuality thus was one of the most tangible domains in which emancipation was acted upon and through which its meanings were expressed. Sovereignty in sexual matters marked an important divide

---

[10]*Angela Y. Davis. Blues Legacies and Black Feminism: Gertrude "Ma" Rainey, Bessie Smith, and Billie Holiday.* NY: Knopf Doubleday, 1999.

between life during slavery and life after emancipation." It arguably remains a singular freedom.

A friend, Terri, told me that she turned to lesbian relationships because she endured so much cruelty from men, and, in particular, the last man she'd been intimate with. Both black, both security guards at a large company, they had sex in the deserted office spaces they patrolled until the night Terri realized he had positioned their bodies in front of a window; she was shocked to see they were being filmed. When she realized that this wasn't the first time he'd done it, she broke up with him and gave up on men. I met Terri while she was in a long-term lesbian relationship. The pair loved and cared for her mate's daughter equally. When they split, they remained friends, shared parenting, loaned each other money and helped each other out. I've seen this dynamic in other black lesbian relations, the split, the sharing of joint resources. I find it noble. Terri died during heart surgery, but during her life she was able to make choices of the heart. Feminist, no?

Like the freed blacks where, as Davis writes, "freely chosen sexual love became a mediator between historical disappointment and the new social realities of an evolving African-American community," modern-day black women are choosing new modes of sex and romance. Terminology reflects how a linguistic understructure impacts the superstructure, e.g. BMW is not a German car but shorthand for Black Man Working. People in the margins of society have appropriated a term of status and economic class, an expensive car, and converted it to instant semiotics to mean *this guy has a job, dude gets a regular paycheck and thus probably his own place, car and feeds himself.* Or, even more significantly, *you don't*

*have to support, shelter, feed and clothe him. You can
enjoy him, have sex free of the dependency that leads
to resentment.*

A wife teaches herself self-love as a virtuous act in
the short story "Dildo" by noted feminist and poet
Toi Derricotte who founded the influential Cave
Canem Foundation for African-American poets.
Her 1992 short-short "Dildo" shows masturba-
tion as a corollary to renunciation and broaches the
unmentionable—a meek, sexually unsatisfied wife,
who is also clever enough to use the US mail to
bring her release:

> She had bought herself a very good-size
> rubber one, molded from an actual erect
> penis....She had quickly brought in the
> box, which was waiting on the front
> steps. Thank God she had beat her hus-
> band and children home....Of course
> she rushed upstairs to try it, and she was
> not disappointed! She was shocked by
> how quickly she responded, and reached
> orgasm—a very deep orgasm—in
> about a minute, even though she hadn't
> touched her clitoris.[11]

Ain't someone a feminist here?

We are beneficiaries of the myriad de facto feminists, armies of them spanning generations, like my
great grandmother, Alice Philyaw, who took magazines and books from her employer's house in the
early 1900s to the colored side of town. Muskogee,
Oklahoma, thus got its First Colored Free Library.

---

[11]Miriam Decosta-Willis, Reginald Martin and Roseann P. Bell, Eds.
Erotique Noire: Black Erotica. NY: Anchor, 1992.

Likeminded de facto feminists are responsible for the proliferation of African-American book clubs, mostly female, that gave mainstream publishing a shot in the arm tantamount to what Black films did for Hollywood between 1968 and 1979.

W.E.B.DuBois said the problem of the 20th century was the problem of the color line.[12] What will this still-new century's problem be? Black people often serve as an early warning system for the American populace; we took the hit first with heroin mid-twentieth century before hard drugs rushed into the mainstream. We've borne the brunt of police brutality, in its myriad forms since enslavement, social media only lately exposing this society's grave mistake in giving the police far greater power than we need them to wield. Freedom fighting's in our DNA. For better and worse, the hardcore issues blacks face — guns, crime, poverty, failing schools — define the newest America.

This country remains an experiment, a photograph developing, its destiny unfurling. The ideal of democracy was contradicted by the inclusion of slavery in the beginning. A Civil War and the Fourteenth and Fifteenth Amendments emancipated blacks. Women got the right to vote as the country urbanized; a century of world wars required all hands on deck. The second wave of feminists occurred as technology and the question of its ownership threw the country into turmoil. Fighting together, separately, at home, in the factory, on mass transportation, being subject to cultural imprinting by television and advertising have made

---

[12]http://sdonline.org/33/du-bois-and-the-question-of-the-color-line-race-and-class-in-the-age-of-globalization/

this nation a hotbed, what public health experts call housing improvised by immigrants or illegal aliens, a dozen people sharing a one-bedroom place, sequentially sharing beds and pillows, their fungal spores contributing to rising tuberculosis rates.

We occupy that hotbed though we prefer to think we each sleep alone. Speaking about the Ebola virus, Pres. Obama recently said: "It is easy to see this as a distant problem until it is not." De facto feminists are not just black women in the United States though the Washington Post study shows the width and breadth of our distance from the mainstream. The future has materialized so suddenly it's often hard to recognize the millions of women being brought out of bondage and ancient oppression around the world.

Terminology makes for binary thinking dilemmas. Are you a suffragette? Patriot? Was Sojourner Truth a feminist? Freedom fighter? Am I black? Or brazen hussy? Both? Perhaps de facto feminists — the lone wolves, lone rangers, lone poets, lone women without whom I can't envision a next wave of feminism — will instruct this world on resourcefulness, sheer grit and mutual aid. It is, after all, not a new phenomenon.

Report from The Front, i.e. Berkeley, CA

Congressman John Lewis, civil rights veteran, and my grandson Jamir, Democratic National Convention 2012

My skateboarding grandson—at 13½ years old just seven months younger than Emmett Till at Till's death—journeyed through time this summer (2015) to visit the International Civil Rights Center & Museum in North Carolina. He and his parents were in Greensboro for a basketball tournament. His mother walked him through the permanent exhibition on the 1960s lunch counter sit-ins—titled The Battlegrounds. Meanwhile, I got free tickets to the new Anna Deavere Smith play, "Notes from the Field: Doing Time in Education, the California Chapter," at the Berkeley Rep. Oh yes, he was born in Berkeley; I was born in Berkeley. Just another week in the life of two natives of that synonym for all things radical—and politically cutting edge—Berkeley.

My friend, who happens to be white, got free tickets to the preview of "Notes from the Field." She was asked by a member of the tech team at The Rep to invite outspoken, passionate, assertive people for the post show discussion. Perfect. How Berkeley can you be?

I screwed on my best "outspoken, passionate, assertive" mindset. After all, this was Anna Deavere Smith whose play, "Fires in the Mirror" on the Watts riots, I flipped over at The Berkeley Rep in 1994. Oh, Watts. Never happen here. The Bay Area. Gay Pride. Chez Panisse. The Black Panthers. My grandson's 4th grade class marched for Cesar Chavez Day. He loves hummus.

USHER BRUTALITY—NOT POLICE BRUTALITY

My friend waits in the lobby for another friend but points three of us (black) upstairs to center front row. The best seats! A white usher, young of course, peers at our tickets and blocks us from our seats. No, no, she says. We're so happy to be there we keep walking and talking. We can see the reserved seats and two friends (black) sitting in them. As soon as we sit down, the usher comes over to get all five of us out of those seats. We point out my friend's name on the reserved signs. The usher's not being very Berkeley. We beg to differ, but stay low key. The theatre has given away 1,000 free tickets and 1,000 half-price tickets for the three-week run to raise awareness about the play's theme, the "school-to-prison pipeline."

Minutes before the show starts I see Fania Davis, executive director of Restorative Justice for Oakland

Youth, with another black woman, frantically trying to locate seats before curtain time. Our usher points the two upwards to the nosebleed section. Oh my, this usher was born long after Fania and her sibling Angela's faces and crowning Afros were instantly recognizable around The Front.

My good friend P. who lives in Alameda—which is like Berkeley but with Victorian houses set on a quaint island—runs her own graphic design company, quite a feat for a colored gal from Watts. She relates her run-in at this very same theatre: "Oh, the irony of it all. I recall a few years back when I went to see another Smith one-woman show there. I was with a group of African-American friends and had to sit one seat away from them because the—white—man who held a season ticket for the seat right next to my friends was there for that performance, and seated. The views from both seats were equally good. I asked him politely (and why would I ask any other way, really?) if he would mind switching seats so I could be next to my friends. To my great surprise, he immediately jumped out of his seat in a rage and mumbled something about he was 'just going to leave' and stormed out. I was shocked. But here's the gravy on the mashed potatoes. After the performance when we went out for after-theatre drinks, my girlfriend told me that right after the incident she overhead two white women seated behind her trying to figure out what had engendered such a violent reaction from the white 'gentleman.' One said to the other 'She must have been militant.'"

A BASTION OF RACISM

Never mind that Ishmael Reed calls our town a "bastion of racism." Never mind that Uncle Ish, esteemed writer/playwright/essayist/poet/professor/ satirist/songwriter/editor and publisher "had a similar experience at the Berkeley Rep. June of 1997," he writes. "At the invitation of Vinnie Burrows, who performed in my play, 'Hubba City' at the Nuyorican Cafe, I'd gone to the Berkeley Rep. to see her and Delores Mitchell star in 'Having Our Say: The Delany Sisters' First 100 years.' A young black man, an employee of the Rep, asked me hostile questions, followed me around and even snooped on me as I talked with the two actresses. It was an uncomfortable experience. However," he says that when he "produced Wajahat Ali's play, 'The Domestic Crusaders' at the Rep. in 2008, the staff cooperated without incident...(Yet) racial profiling is rampant in Berkeley."

Now, now, Uncle Ish, not in Berkeley. On this grand night of free seats distributed like government cheese to presentable Negroes, I sit amongst a legion of people of color. Far more than I see when I get my customary last-minute no-show seat for Culture Clash's sociopolitical satire. Even then, I count fewer faces of color than I have fingers — on one hand. Outside, Berkeley remains a tale of two cities. At the university and the hillsides, the flood of Asian students and foreign students colorize Cal like an unfinished portrait. Very little charcoal or, as Crayola dubs it, fuzzy wuzzy brown. In the flatlands, brown, black and white co-exist. Of the city's roughly 320,000 residents, 13.2% are African-Americans. The homeless, with worldly goods spilling from shopping carts and ever-present signs, form a strategic border of begging protecting upscale Berkeley from common mortal Berkeley. The Berkeley Rep sits evenly on this border. When I was a girl, Berkeley was segregated. Blacks could only swim in the municipal pool on Friday night. And the stores had to be integrated by protestors from CORE.

But Berkeley has been to integration what lace is to lingerie, and white liberalism could not possibly conceal leftover bigotry. Or could it? Is prejudice like Godzilla? No matter how many times we legislate it away, Supreme Court-it away, affirmative-action it away, talk it to death, it rises ingloriously, like the radiated monster.

Mornings on University Ave, the frontline of The Front, the newsstands brim with NY Times, Wall Street Journal, SF Chron, Oakland Trib, and free papers including East Bay Express. The streets are awash with every kind of transport — cars, buses, bicyclists, toddlers in low-wheelies attached to bikes, joggers with strollers — everything except horses and rickshaws. Uncle Ish goes for his usual morning espresso. This particular day he had a meeting with the officers of his arts foundation in the section where they serve lunch. As soon as Uncle Ish entered the area, a Hispanic waiter shouted at him, rudely asking him what he wanted.

Can a brother get some respect? The waiter must have confused Uncle Ish with the legion of homeless brothers out here, some of whom have mental problems. Uncle Ish is gray and bearded, a commonplace in Berkeley. Uncle Ish says this is not the only place that blacks in Berkeley have been quarantined. I love Uncle Ish's language, quarantined, bastion.

For the meantime, another Berkeley Rep usher, this time black and female, walks over and says, "Folks, you have to move, these seats are reserved." She pulls out that mama-ain't-playing-with-you tone; we stay firm. No matter we're professional, fifties+, spiffed up and law abiding. Don't matter. We might as well be Henry Louis Gates breaking into his own home in Cambridge. She has the same tone that Herman Cain, last seen running away from the Presidential Sweepstakes, took in his interviews. I seem to hear it from Ben Carson, when he scolds Obama or offers "common-sense prescriptions." It's hard to play at gestapo without Uncle Tom tonality.

It takes another few minutes for my friend to appear with her cheery face, and magically the ushers cease and desist. It was all a glitch. Our seats were reserved for the tech crew, and no one had communicated that to the front of the house. We proceed to enjoy the play, if enjoy still applies to collisions at The Front between generations, races and attitudes. At play's end, Anna Deavere Smith bows and graciously pulls Fania Davis up from her front row seat and kisses her ceremoniously. I guess the ushers got that one wrong too.

I jabber about the incident in an open letter to the playwright and the company on Facebook setting out the sequence of events. Two local papers The Daily Californian and East Bay Express pick up the post. It becomes the controversy, and Berkeley Rep calls — after much internal talk, its director of marketing says — and apologizes. I ask for a formal letter of apology. She wants to know if I have any suggestions. Yes, offer more plays with ethnic and black writers, continue to give out free tickets, train everybody in diversity, pair productions with The

Lower Bottom Playaz and other community based theaters. I mention Elizabeth Warren's clarion call to the upper classes, that they don't own the bounty of this society nor merit it. And I remind her of TOBA, Theater Owners Booking Agency, informally known as Tough on Black Asses, that booked black acts in the south in the 1900s until artists like Lena Horne and jazz musicians broke the color barrier. It's not enough for Anna Deavere Smith to come for three weeks and leave, and BRT to go back to biz as usual.

The Rep sends me a formal *if we've offended you, we're sorry apology*, adding that their audiences are 20% people of color. A friend who is a UC prof and season subscriber at the Rep scoffs at the 20% number. She and others say audiences are nearly all-white as I've seen. This kind of incident is not an anomaly. African-American entrepreneurs, intellectuals and artisans have long been the target of hostility and terror in this country. Many black shopkeepers were lynched by outraged and economically dispossessed white Southerners. Black Wall Street, one of the nation's most affluent all-Black communities, in Tulsa, Oklahoma, was burned down in 1921 by angry white residents. Many people are unaware that the terrorist bomb attack on the Alfred P. Murrah Federal Building in downtown Oklahoma City in 1995 wiped out a solid bloc of the city's black middle class who were civil service workers. My family is from Oklahoma; my aunt, a librarian and prominent soror, moved from Oklahoma City after the bombing, distraught at the loss of so many in her community.

Home from his travels to the South, my grandson and his parents found shocking that the white drinking fountains had been a nickel whilst the coloreds' cost a dime. Ah, those darned public accommodations. If only they were not symptomatic of deeper issues. I imagine the pictures from Greensboro in my grandson's head as he bikes around our lovely hometown…Berkeley. In spite of the loveliness, his summer travels have an impact. He brings up Emmett Till, puzzled why he was murdered so brutally for looking at a white girl. This would never happen in Berkeley, he says. On social media, he gets a headshot from a white classmate. We see it. And we don't see it. Then she sends a second, glammed up picture we do not ignore. We have The Talk, the Emmett Till talk, the sexting talk, the Instagram talk. Yes, there are many versions of The Talk. Being young and black is precarious, even in Berkeley — or should I say, especially in Berkeley — where one can forget the rules and suffer the consequences.

Acknowledge Me:
a true ghost story/epistolary essay/postmodern spiritual narrative

(Real people's names, where necessary, have been changed)

In December of 2006, I opened up The New York Times to find that two great artists whose lives had thoroughly informed mine had died. One was James Brown, King of R&B, whose music I've loved since childhood. I mourned him in a thoroughly appropriate way, blasting his greatest hits while exercising to a fare-thee-well.

Then there was Peter Thorpe, Broadway playwright and artistic director of the fabled The Repertory theater company. Peter had befriended me during a short but intense course in playwriting in New York City in 1985. We corresponded infrequently until we lost contact when he moved west and became a successful screenwriter.

Mucking around on Myspace I found a tribute to Peter by another theater acolyte. I poured out my feelings to him because he seemed as affected by Peter as I was. The very next day, much to my surprise, Peter's wife responded to my tribute in a personal message, obviously in tears.

We began a dialogue or should I say a trialogue: Alexis on the phone, me e-mailing and Peter, hmmm, Peter in the great space.

March 19, 2007

Dear Alexis,

I am so sorry for your loss of Peter. He was one of the greats.
When I read his obituary in the New York Times, I hadn't seen
him in forever, so I held my tears. But it kept at me, and finally I
cried over the loss to the world of such a heartfelt, perceptive
person. I've been in theater since taking his class in '85 and not
encountered his likes again, to my dismay.

So, finally, I told myself to buckle up and do something practical
to honor what Peter taught me. I decided to read every one
of Peter's plays. I ordered them over the Internet. Something
mystical happened. Please don't read on if you think this might
upset you.

Last year, from January through May, I wrote a play called
Theodicy, about two older black men at a river who accidentally fall into the river of death. They talk about their lives, their
careers and their belief/non-belief in a God who permits such
tremendous suffering in the world. Oba, a retired eye doctor,
has gone blind and in a wheelchair because he lost a leg to
diabetes. They travel back in time through his beloved black
history where Oba confronts many scenes, including a long
one in the Civil War.

I received Peter's play *Influence* a week before the second
staged reading of mine. Though dead tired, I read it all the way
through, finding so much of Peter there. I went to sleep and
woke up like lightning had hit—he's got two guys sitting by a
river, one in a wheelchair, yakking on and on about their career
highlights. How could this be?

Then my director called to say my stage directions were con-
fusing...could I do something?

Peter once told our class he was a director first, then a writer,
and that's where he learned how to handle things onstage. So
I used Peter's opening stage directions in *Influence* for *Theodicy*.
Right after I typed the stage directions on my computer, a burst
of thunder as loud as a plane crashing, rumbled in the sky, and
everything got deleted. I love all manner of mystical stuff. I had
to smile. A friend told me it was the universe reaching down
and giving me a helping hand.

My father was a Taurus and when Peter found that out, he
laughed and told me he was a stubborn-ass Taurus too. He
loved the character in my play for his class that was based on
my father, a crusty, streetwise type. I wrote a shout-out in the

play to my dad and Peter. I am sure they are exchanging war stories, westerns and murder mysteries somewhere up there.

Peter was more than special, much more.

with deep appreciation, Faith

> *Alexis said your dad lost his leg to diabetes. She also said she's finding life impossible without you. And that I helped her heart.*

March 20, 2007

Dear Alexis,

The LA Times obit which goes so in-depth on Peter's accomplishments is illuminating.

Our class was for writers from other genres who wanted to write a play. I was the sole poet in the group. There were three or four from Saturday Night Live, a pair of novelists, a Merv Griffin writer who called Peter from deep sea fishing in Maui when he couldn't make it to class, plus screenwriters, sitcom writers, etc. Most had already reached a $$$ zenith for writers and kvetched over whether the New York Times could review any play they wrote without knocking their TV/screen background.

Not a struggling artist type in the bunch except for me, and I could barely afford the 200 bucks to take the course. But I worked my tail off—it pretty much got to the point that every week Peter would say, "So who else has a scene besides Faith?" I was just learning the craft, but Peter took a shine to my work and "protected" me throughout the course. I never forgot his kindness.

I'm a native of Berkeley and returned to Oakland in 1990, so I'd love to jump down to LA and come to a celebration of life for Peter. I'm traveling to the East Coast in early June, so NYC is also a possibility. Please do inform me of the dates and times.

Thank you for including the picture. It's an absolute delight to see Peter with a golden California tan, in such high spirits and still so youthful. Somehow, "talking" to you and seeing the picture has made me feel better about Peter. I still get angry at the thought of his going.

With love and sympathy, Faith

Hang in there. I know grief. It's a valuable emotion.

My poem for my parents whose illnesses brought me home to California:

in sickness and in health

as I held my father's hand
his doctor catheterized him
he rallied and got better but
there is no privacy in sickness.

when we revisited the stainless
steel sickroom he motioned me
to leave the room
before the procedure but

there is no privacy in sickness. Later
her memory going, I help mom's legs
onto the stainless gurney, shocked
at the beauty of her smooth

still black-haired crotch, at the two
who in complete and utter privacy
made me. health is an open secret
but in sickness there is no privacy.

When I told her about the class, Alexis said your take
on it—"Who else has a scene besides Faith"—is
quintessential you.

March 21, 2007

Alexis,

That class was at the Writers Community in a brownstone on East 89th. At a poetry course with Carolyn Forché, the program administrator casually asked if anyone wanted to write a play. I was the only one. I had written a ten-minute, but knew I needed direction. Peter's class was surreal. Every week on my walk from the subway, I passed Diana Ross' three little girls playing tag and hopscotch next to their chauffeured stretch limo outside the Dalton School.

The most self-important person in the class let it be known that Hollywood had anointed him the next Carl Reiner. He went into his shtick about his love of the Dick Van Dyke Show, how he'd wanted to be a comedy writer ever since seeing that show, how he'd even found a wife who looked just like Mary Tyler Moore, blah blah blah…yeah, he had gotten hold of the brass ring, so more power to him. Schmuck from the word go.

The guy from Merv Griffin's show had just finished the ump-teenth-year run. The lowest self-projection, what we've come to call self-esteem, in the book. But he knew how to enjoy his $$$. Peter would have such a cynical smirk when he would tell us how this guy called in from Hawaii where he'd gone deep sea fishing instead of writing his scene.

The one that got on Peter's nerves the most was a ladies-who lunch-type. Straight out of West Orange, NJ. Money, money, money. And one day she comes in screaming, "I just got a $25,000 advance for my novel." Peter almost shit on himself. He made some comment like, I bet it's a women's lib theme. I felt like shaking him and saying, why ever would you be jealous of any of these people? They're here because they want what you've already got—a Broadway play and a serious rep.

And then there was the little sad girl writer from Saturday Night Live (are you laughing yet?), so depressed. I don't know why. Maybe the boys—Chevy, John Belushi—gave her a hard time. And another blowhard was this guy who let everybody know "Hollywood has called me." He came in leather/sueded down every week. Actually he was good-looking New York all the way, Italian stallion type, and he would throw down his folder with a big slam on the table, sort of like to announce, "I'm here but this class is just bullshit, pure schmooze. I have a big career." But he did say one week, "Just my luck. I write a movie for Clint Eastwood and Burt Reynolds. And it's Clint's only flop." (I hope none of these people are your friends, but if they are, tell them I can't help it if they were assholes 22 years ago.)

So anyway, missy, I hope you got a laugh or two today. You gotta try for a laugh a day, if you have to laugh through your tears. I would have gone off the deep end myself without my sense of humor.

love, Faith

March 23, 2007

Alexis,

I'm writing this Friday morning, early a.m., putting it in draft because Peter is yakking at me and I have to get it down. I didn't want to bother you.

I've been having a lot of problems sleeping with these things physically gripping me in the night, night visitations. I wonder why I'm feeling Peter's death so much, when I hadn't seen him in so long. I tried to find him on the internet about two years ago but gave up.

So my friend told me to tell these spirits to be open and frank with me about what they want: So I thought, it's Peter, and I said, what do you want? And Peter said, *hurry up and get the play done. Do the revisions but make them brief. Stop dicking around. Get the show on the road.* And he also said to tell you that he and I never had an affair, that he was a gentleman around me, no hanky-panky, but there was a sexual attraction. *Good heavens, I'm only human and you should see her tatas.*

Alexis, I dunno. This is what I heard. I was enormously drawn to Peter, but I knew it was for his kindness and recognition of me...and he was way too mature for me and my goofy-silly stuff.

I thought about not sending this in the car today. I just thought you're going to think it's too weird, but right away, Peter said, tell her—and he called you *Alexis, my sweet.*

I did psychic stuff in the 60s/70s until it got trendy and phony and I stopped. But **I'm from Berkeley**. I retained my intuition...wouldn't be alive without it.

love, Faith

> *Okay, I told her. She said you guys were into psychics all along.*

March 24, 2007

Oh Alexis,

I'm so glad you weren't offended. It was a chance but a logical one, given our prior communications. Peter is talking a lot. This morning as I was scrubbing my tub and getting ready for teaching my class, I asked, *what is this all about and how long are you gonna be around???!!*

And he said, *I'm going to hound you day and night until you become a successful writer*

I said, *oh boy, and how long is that going to take?*

He said, *it's gonna happen sooner than you think*

I said, *well, thanks, I mean where were you for the last ten years?*

He said, *I didn't have time. Now I have all the time in the world. And I have the resources of the universe at my disposal!*

And we talked about confidence and talent, and he said it's better to have talent than confidence...and he just now added, *you can fake confidence but you can't fake talent*

So after I got your reply, I remembered that I had put on a post-it note maybe right after I read his obit: *Peter Thorpe, How cd u check out? I thought you had special powers —*

And I never removed it from my dresser in my bedroom. I think it had some effect. So, Alexis, I think you should write Peter a note with a question on it. I also did what you said, telling him what you said: "I love him and he can visit me anytime." I think you need to say it out loud, with attitude, and talk to him directly. God, I feel like Whoopi Goldberg in *Ghost*. But I know this stuff is real.

much love, Faith

March 25, 2007

Alexis,

Peter is yakking at me. I told him I don't feel like telling you
all this, but he said: *It's **absolutely** important. Be a person
of integrity.* And he also said: *get up, lazybones.* And he com-
mended me on the revisions I did yesterday and said I'm almost
through. And I've got to respond to the guy who asked to see
my plays. He said sarcastically: how many theater directors have
asked to see your plays anyway?

Peter said for you to check the records or papers, insurance,
taxes, and that you have to dig deep, but it's necessary to get
dates and figures right. He kept stressing this. He said this is the
way you are going to dig out of the depression — by taking care
of records, papers, etc. (and I got a visual of you digging near
a rose bush or something trellised, possibly I was picking up
something from the photo).

Oh, I also keep a record of my dreams. Kind of more informal,
even though it's best to record a dream as soon as I wake up.
Anyway, the dream that's behind all of this was January 7th. I saw
Peter in an outside classroom full of people. The sun was so
bright it was almost blinding and Peter smiled at me from the
front of the crowd like I was his star pupil. I woke up crying.
That's when I realized how deeply his death had impacted me.

Peter's also very funny. I asked why he talks to me so much in
the bathroom, and he said: why do you think? *I like being in the
bathroom with women.* And he got even raunchier.

Last night, I talked to my good friend Janis in New Jersey, who
was nearly speechless. She said Peter and I are "in the same
mental energy field."

my love, Faith

> *Why are you always here when I'm in the
> bathroom?*
>> *There's nothing more of a turn-on
>> than a woman taking a crap*

March 25, 2007

Alexis,

Okay. Here goes. This is Sunday morning, and again it's weird
and I don't want to upset or bombard you. But Peter says you
need upsetting to get out of the deep grief. He said grief is ok
but he doesn't want you to hurt yourself.

Peter told me to make up my bed. My dad and I argued
throughout my teen years about this because I said, why make
it up when I just have to get back in it at night?

Peter said I need to make up my bed so no other ghosts (that's
the word I heard) can get in it during the day.

Then he said tell you to get up and make up your bed every
day **tightly** as soon as you rise. Peter said, you're vulnerable,
and it's not other men he's worried about, it's other spirits.

love, Faith

> Why aren't you going back to her?
>> She can't see me
> The veil of tears?
>> She has to get through that
> Are you saying dead people don't want us to mourn them?
>> Tears, ok
> A flood
>> For months? She's got too much business
>> to take care of

March 25, 2007

Alexis,

This morning, Peter said: *go visit your mother* **today**. I hadn't
been in weeks because of the plays, traveling, etc. I had a busy
day this morning but managed to see her. She's 87 and has
Alzheimer's. Today of all days, her friend from her church was
there with her daughter, my good friend from adolescence
that I hadn't talked to in decades. Just pure serendipity and a
great visit.

I agree with you: "...how fascinating it is that we've met this
way. Some things that I'm sharing with you, I haven't shared
with anyone."

When I did psychic stuff before, our society was open and
free thinking. It's closed since, and I wrote to you with great

183

trepidation. Thank you for your expression of gratitude and for respecting me.

I definitely understand your concern with your voice, your life. I'm fairly giving so always have to give **myself** time — usually through my hour of daily chanting. Otherwise I get overwhelmed and clogged with other people's emotions. Alexis, this is not selfish. When you said that you really can't continue unless you find your voice again, I recognized caretaker fatigue.

I got it after helping my Dad through his terminal illness and then working with my mom being widowed, then dementia and the early stages of Alzheimer's when I lived with her.

Finally my sister and I had to put her in a local nursing home where she lived for three years before she had a stroke in October. Now she requires a smaller home-style situation. Once my sis and I no longer split caring for her, I needed to take care of Faith. I had to say no a lot to recharge my batteries.

Last fall, after four years with my son, his girlfriend and my adorable grandson, I had to discontinue Baby Night which was like Sunday dinner at Grandma's. They squabbled and acted out so badly that, one night, I packed the food, gave it to them in a big shopping bag, and basically said, I love you but work out your relationship away from me, not in front of me. Whew! Talk about the sandwich generation.

So carve out your time right now, an hour in the morning, whatever, that's just for you. Here's one thing I did once we placed my mom: I took the phone out of my bedroom. Friends, children, relatives even acquaintances will call at all hours. Calls after 10 are almost always a request to listen to a problem, get something, and do something. It's cut down on stress. This particular change may not be for you — but look around and see where you can cut over-giving.

When bad people give out, nobody misses them. When good people give out, it's hard on everybody. So it's better for good people to learn how to preserve themselves.

Thank you so much for our exchange.

with much love, Faith

p.s. here's natural stuff to counteract depression: tryptophan, fish oil, Magnesium citrate, B-calm, Sunshine; vitamin D3. I have my bouts with depression, but have such a sensitive system that I avoid prescription meds. I use a lot of St. John's Wort and try to eat healthy.

> *You're a healer. Stop tripping*
> *Meaning what, O Great One?*
> > *You help people get over rough spots*
> *I have a soft shoulder*
> > *I see it with you and your friends*
> *Especially my friends*
> > *It's why you like to chant*
> *I chant for other people all the time*
> > *You told Joyce that you chanted more for*
> > *your ex and his wife than anyone*
> *Heaven only knows*
> > *And Joyce said there's some lesson you're*
> > *getting from that*
> *If he's happy and she's happy, I'm happy*
> > *That's the wounded healer*

March 26, 2007

Hi Alexis,

You sound better, livelier. I'm feeling that way too. I recorded in my journal last night, and as I looked, I realized that we've been doing this back and forth for one week!! My gosh, what we've done and where we went in one week—amazing.

In class, I always sat next to Peter and he used to put his hand on my forearm as if to steady me, as if he knew how unsure I was underneath being a big pop-off at the mouth.

I've felt that same steadying effect for a while now from him.

This morning, I got up and felt good that perhaps you and I accomplished stuff and did some of what Peter wanted. I drove with a friend Kay to find out about free money for a condo. And as we're traveling down the highway looking at the green expanse of hills, I realized Peter was with us. I said in my mind, what are you, some kind of Jiminy Cricket on my shoulder?

And Peter said *you have an interesting life.*

Well, Kay and I were having a great conversation about karma, and she asked did I have late karma because we each had known about this freebie for a while. We discussed how we've tackled our karma over the years as Buddhists.

And Peter was like *that's why you had to grow up more to get in theater. You can't be late for theater.*

And then Kay and I were in the mortgage broker's office talking about why it had taken so long to get to first-home buying. I realized it's because for everything I really want, deep down inside I think I can't do it. It takes so much effort.

Peter was checking out all the requirements the broker gave us to fill out to get this deal: W-2 forms, 2005–2006 taxes, 401K plans, bank statements. And he said: see *what I was talking about? Papers, taxes, records. I wasn't just talking about Alexis. It's you too.*

And on the way back, Kay and I drove by many businesses along the highway. One stood out: ThorpeWiseGuides. Peter laughed and said *that's why I came along.*

And in the bathroom earlier, he said, *I'm your friend.* And he keeps saying *your father's right.* And he said *I want you to meet Alexis soon, can you go down next week?*

This is out there, Alexis, but I'm here for the ride.

Faith

> *Peter, you can sleep on the sofa.*
>> *Oh no, this is the best part*
> *Going to sleep with me?*
>> *All kinds of stuff happens once you fall asleep*
>> *Turn toward me so we can snuggle*
> *I need to get off*
>> *It's ok*
>> *I've been inside you while you've done it*
>> *Remember the hotel?*
>> *In Minneapolis?*
> *That was way before Alexis' first e-mail.*
> *I was at the theater conference*
> *The first of March. Peter! You've been hanging around me all this time?*
>> *Yeah*
>> *I've been here awhile*
> *Since the night when I broke down and cried and had the dream about you?*
>> *Yeah*

March 27, 2007

Dear Alexis,

Thank you for even asking to read *Theodicy*. Peter really helped me in a surprising way. Yesterday after hanging with me all day, it seemed he came to my chanting meeting. I often chant for my relatives or friends who are troubled and imagine them sitting next to me. So I did that with Peter, as I have since reading his obit. The most incredible thing happened. First I saw him as an adult next to me—then he turned into a tot and sat in my lap. And stayed that way all evening, and I was the lead chanter.

He proceeded to tell me about being a child and getting beaten about the head with a shoe and his mother putting Mercurochrome on it. I was so shocked. And didn't know what to make of it. At bedtime, the tiny invisible boy insisted on sleeping with me. He said *I'm so small, I won't take up any room*. I said, ok, no problem, and curled up and had a great sleep until 3am.

I awoke and decided to work on the revision (and had completely forgotten the boy). Well, when I came to the end of the play where there's a little boy, I could see that the image I had at night belonged in the play.

Can you believe this? My imagination has always driven people wild. I had an invisible red chicken as a child which needed a seat on the bus or car or I would scream bloody murder, but mostly I learned to keep it to myself, as in **rich inner life**, ho ho ho.

This is not the kind of thing that you can tell people, if you know what I mean. I too am looking forward to seeing you.

Love, Faith

510-xxx-xxxx; I'm usually home early afternoon.

    don't tell Alexis everything

March 27, 2007

Alexis,

I just thought about shape shifters in literature after the experience last night. You know, I only knew Peter as a mature successful mentor, not as anything else. I went on line to find out more about psychic experiences with the deceased.

I began to wonder: Is this getting dangerous? Is he stuck here? Did he pick me because I'm so open that I'm a sieve? All day, I've been telling him: Peter, go home, go see your dogs, Peter, why are you here? He answered but I can't remember. Still tired from finishing the revision.

So I found this site which had some answers that made sense to me: http://www.psychiccourses.com/faqs.php

"What are the 'cool breeze' and the feeling that someone is present and watching?" It's the people who have died and left this earthly plane to join the other side. When they wish to communicate with us they choose different methods based on the person receiving the information. *Some will turn up in person and others will make a 'phone call'. The phone call can be described as similar to long distance phone calls before satellite. There is a short delay before messages are received. When a spirit turns up in person they will communicate nearly always telepathically.*

"The 'cool breeze' commonly felt upon entering certain rooms, a place, or building often indicates when spirits are present. When a person dies it is as though a cord that connects them to the earth plane is cut. They slip out and pass to the 'other side'. Some are caught between the two and remain bound to the earth, therefore becoming earthbound spirits, or ghosts. When spirits wish to communicate regardless of whether they have successfully passed over, the room temperature may appear to drop. This is because our vibrational density is thicker on this side and they have to draw on the earth's energy to maintain their physical presence when visiting. The 'breeze' is often because you have walked straight through them! If you 'feel' a presence, it usually is exactly that. Someone from the other side wants to talk with you!"

I went to a job interview yesterday to be a resident artist for a small theatre company for children. The director said I'd have to use the program's theme in the residencies I'm assigned. The theme is Ghosts! I got the job. Peter was in the room and was saying *this is small potatoes, don't be intimidated by her.*

I'm not scared, but I like to keep problems small by understanding them and being cautious.

love, Faith

March 28, 2007

Alexis,

Thank you for your kindness.

I have a wild imagination that I have been able to tap creatively. Nonetheless, as a child, my mom had to work with me because of nightmares, sleepwalking, mild hysteria, seeing things, etc. which persisted well into adulthood. I was very fearful to sleep alone until I was in my 30s. My ex said when my head hit the pillow, I talked in my sleep, saw things and people, the whole nine yards.

So the edges blurring is an appropriate call. And I have been very tired, working almost maniacally and getting into a trance-like state to finish this revision of the play. A combination which increases my susceptibility to wilder thought patterns.

I'm sorry where I offended. I do not want to put you through anything disquieting. Tomorrow evening after 5:45 I should be home. Maybe we can talk then.

with love and much respect, Faith

p.s. I live a fairly straight life; this side of me doesn't surface except for my writing and a zany humor. But, as you know from reading the e-mails, it's not all humorous. After seeing this side of someone, and to call that person dear, even if you've only known me one week, comforts me. thank you.

> *You need to give me some slack because I can't do*
> *what you do.*
> > *Why not?*
> *I'm not a white male*
> > *Some of this isn't about white or male*
> > *It's on you*
> > *Faith*
> > *The writer*
> > *The woman*
> > *The wannabe*

March 28, 2007

Alexis,

Peter said yesterday to open the ledger—I'm seeing a big green ledger—and start working on it. He said just go to the ledger by the armchair near the window. I'm seeing you curled up in a tufted leather chair working on it.

He's still here. I did as you said and nudged him to go to you. He said *I'm having fun.* I said, but Alexis needs you. All he said was *Big mama.* He kept repeating *Big mama Big mama.*

Then he said he was afraid of your wrath. He said there's so much work to do. And you're going to be mad at how much is on your shoulders. He said he was sorry about it.

Last night as I got in bed, he was there, stretched out. I have a thing about closed doors when I sleep. Peter said *don't worry about the door. It's closed enough.* I turned over to face the outside of the bed. And Peter said: *turn over and face me. It's all right; this is not sexual.* He said *I'm feeling relaxed.*

He has made a lot of cracks about my finances like, like calling them *Faith's nonfinances. Bank account? What bank account—there's nothing in it.* And this morning he said, *you're not a struggling artist anymore. You're an accomplished writer. Being this broke is not good. It's bad. I'm here to help you.*

And he also said anybody, including and especially you, can tell what kind of a person I am by what I write. So why do I always try to hide it?

with love, Faith

> *You have to work harder on cleaning*
> Okay, Mr. Clean. Did you notice I cleaned my silverware drawer?
> *For the first time in how many years?*
> A decade. Sorry, sorry, sorry.
> *Notice how your friends always bring their own water?*
> Everybody does.
> *Their own food?*
> So?
> *And their own eating utensils?*
> Why do they even come?
> *Because you're a healer*
> A wounded one, right?
> *Right*

190

March 30, 2007

Hi Alexis,

Hope you're feeling ok. Just a postscript on our conversation and events of yesterday. My friend Joyce called me tonight. When she entered the room where we were chanting, Peter went *Big Mama! That's what I was talking about*. And he followed after her like Richard Pryor and Gene Wilder in that prison comedy. Tonight Joyce said she was chuckling about it during the day and remembered that her deceased grandmother was called Big Mama, and that she's always felt her protective presence throughout her life.

??Who knows?? Maybe Peter and Big Mama got acquainted in "the great space" —

Also my friend Marta and I went to the theater and saw a new play at ACT in SF. I pretty much thought Peter had left because I wasn't picking up anything during the play from him. Then this morning, while Marta and I were having our chanting session and talking about the play, which we did not like and found much fault with, Peter said very plainly, *No comment*. I told Marta, and he repeated, *No comment*. We thought that was a scream and a wry way of saying he agreed with us.

Have a nice weekend. Our weather is finally getting mellow.

love, Faith

> *Peter, I need to masturbate. It's kind of uncomfortable*
> *with you here.*
>> *I can't see*
>> *Do you think I took my eyes with me?*
>> *Death is weightlessness*
> *I keep seeing you as a young man for some reason.*
>> *I'm not going anywhere*
>> *I like it here*
>> *I love your music and when you get up and*
>> *dance*
>> *All the rhythm inside your brain*
>> *Yr heart*
>> *And when you masturbate…it's perfect*
>> *I really like the theater director fantasy*
>> *Intensely pleasurable*

March 31, 2007

Alexis,

Peter said to tell you to use the totem pole approach, you'd know what he meant. And he mentioned the Family of Man photo exhibit from '55. I vaguely remember it. Don't know what it means. Maybe you have the book and something important is sitting next to it, or a photo from it will trigger something else.

I got real busy, but he's been hanging with me. He loves my friends. He repeatedly says Marta is a smart little cookie. She's Latina/native American and a Ph.D. in statistics, but can't get her worth. She's an aspiring playwriter, and is reading "Aristotle's Poetics for Screenwriters." Peter said: *how come she has this and you don't?*

love, Faith

> *I'm a little nuts.*
> > *That's cool*
> *Thank you.*
> > *You're welcome*
> *I write like a wizard. I get started and go, go, go.*
> > *Just stop being maniacal*
> > *Writing is a profession*
> > *Get up*
> > *Eat breakfast*
> > *Write*
> > *Stop*
> > *Live*

April 2, 2007

Hi Alexis,

I keep saying to myself, is this imagination or is this really happening? I said to Peter: why is this happening? And he said: *don't ask me that one more time.* Then later, like an hour or so, he said: *we're from the same tribe.*

That blew me away. I had been reading about the beginning of nation-states and how all the problems in the world started when we went from tribes to nation-states with, in a sense, manufactured animosities, not the more natural fights between the tribes.

So Peter also said: cut the Alice-in-Wonderland act. It's affecting your writing... you can't write innocence forever. He's been giving me extended tutorials on writing.

Also he's been giving me glimpses into the world and the universe. He gets around all of it very easily, in and out, around and here and there. He said: our world is so small, just a tiny part of the great space. I told you on the phone that he said death is weightlessness. It's absolutely no big deal for him to access inside anybody, outside. Wow, what a phantasmagoria. He also said the forces are arrayed in space watching the Bush-Iran-Iraq thing, kind of like this is no big deal, idiots take care of themselves in due time.

During the chanting, which he loves and is pleased that I light incense for him, Peter asked: why aren't you chanting more for the dead Panthers? I was in the Black Panther Party in my youth. He said I would be able to help them and help myself finish/revise my novel about that period if I wrote the names of the dead down and prayed more for them, including Huey and Eldridge. He said they need my prayers.

He was here when my good friend R. came over. She has a fear of flying and wants to go to a reunion in LA, but can't because of her fear. After she left, Peter said he could help her overcome her fear instantly. He said, *tell her.* I didn't want to because she is super-grounded and materialistic, but he insisted.

So last night I told her that my spirit guy could help her. She just said she thought it was weird. So I said to Peter after she and I hung up: so why tell her if she's just going to weird out on me? And he said: **you** *need to know which of your friends is receptive to this. Tell her anyway that I said her fear is not of airplanes but of airports. If you can get her to an airport, we can help her.*

love, Faith

> *I love the little Latina*
Marta?
> > *Yeah, I like the laughter and sense of community you*
> > *have with her and Joyce and the other Buddhists*
> *Yeah, we yuk it up while we're confronting the four*
> *sufferings — birth, old age, illness and death.*
> > *When you have them over, you clean up your house*
> *I call it cleaning for the Buddha.*
> > *You have to work a rhythm of cleanliness*

I get into a frenzy of cleaning for guests.
Why can't you work like that for yourself?
Aren't you a Buddha?

April 2, 2007

Alexis,

You might want to go to the New Yorker, the 3.19.07 issue. I read the fiction by Jonathan Lethem. Peter thought the story was a gas, made me read it to the end.

Also in a dream, the green ledger appeared again. First it was a book that Peter had written; then, when I opened it, it turned out to be a book of hymns and poems. At the end of the book was a detailed Thorpe family history written by his mother Ellie. I couldn't figure that out.

Peter is really on me about cleanliness. I let things go when I'm writing, then get very irritable when things are a mess. So back to the soothing rhythm of cleaning and washing.

love, Faith

> *Faith, having a filthy house is what's*
> *stopping you*
> *You write in frenzy until the filth*
> *overtakes you*
> *Then you drop everything and clean like there's no*
> *tomorrow*

It's called being human, something you don't know anymore.

> *When you drop and clean you lose the thread. And*
> *because you have so many stories in your head, so*
> *much dialogue*
> *so much gossip and history, when you switch projects*
> *you lose momentum*

What do you know? You had a wife, a houseboy, house-
keeper, 125 thou a week to keep you going.

> *And loved every penny of it.*
> *I worked my way up to top dog in Hollywood*

What a cliché. You got to top dog in Hollywood with
that shit?

> *I knew how to use the cliché moment*

I thought multitasking my projects was good?

> *But don't switch at 90 miles an hour*
> *Switch when you come to a stop*

Thank you, Peter.

> *Been a while since I heard you say that*
>
> Dead white men make me sick. On my dollar or on my collar.
>
> > *You're the picture of health*
>
> I was reading The New Yorker *article about Roberto* Bolaño *when I realized you were reading alongside me.*
>
> > *You have to learn how to read and discard, write and discard*
>
> You mean disregard?
>
> > *No. Discard. Bolaño wrote a 200 page novel*
>
> Are you saying my 600 page magnum opus isn't cool?
>
> > *You have to learn how to write to length*
>
> What does that mean, Mr. Big Authority in the Sky?
>
> > *Edit like this:*
> > *cut when the scene's done what you wanted*
> > *cut character when he's said what you wanted*
> > *cut*
> > *cut*
> > *cut*

April 3, 2007

Alexis,

I'm glad that these letters are an upper for you. I often reread our exchanges. And Peter just said reading them is an immense source of joy for him, that he loves you dearly, and wants everything to work out fine.

I went to visit another friend B. and I told her about the plays and Peter. She's from Hong Kong and a poet. She told me of the belief in her culture that a deceased person sometimes stays earthbound because of unfinished business. Peter agreed: *I **told** you telling your friends about me is important.*

After I left B's, Peter and I had a very serious conversation. We've had a running argument about Peter's being a white male and having advantages, and my being a black female and struggling harder. Peter doesn't give me one ounce of slack on that, and when I told that to Joyce—black, female and a high achiever—she agreed with Peter, that my life is about the limitations of Faith. Which of course I have enough wisdom to understand, and know far too many highly successful blacks to claim it as a serious argument.

Peter and I fuss because he's so demanding. And it's embarrassing to have someone know the inside of my life so intimately and see how deflated and alone I've been feeling in this past year or so, just when my plays have been getting on. I keep up the bravest front.

So Peter and I discuss fame, success, acclaim, money, ambition, and the lengths one has to go to get any of that. I can't remember a lot of it because we're in the car. Peter just loves to ride and zip down the freeway. He jabbers on, but my feeling of being embarrassed led me to tell him I don't know if he's real or just my imagination. His response: *That's sad.* He's made that observation about my life several times. That it's sad but he's here to help. I told him I get tired. It's been a long road, this life as a writer.

I'm sorry that this is not zany or funny but, like you said, it comes in waves.

Peter said: *This is the core of what's held you back as a writer, the unwillingness to confront the sadness. If you're sad, you're sad. You have the ability to write funny. That's great. That's rare. But you also have the eye to see human suffering, and you tend to stay away from it. Confront it. It won't kill you.*

Whew! Peter Thorpe, a hell of a mentor. I asked him one day: I thought you were just a playwriting mentor. How come you're so concerned about all these areas of my life? And he said a real mentor is concerned about every aspect of his pupil's life.

much love, Faith

April 5, 2007

Hi Alexis,

Dear sweet Peter has had me hopping still. He's been a bugbear about multitasking, says since I can read nine different books and mags because I want to, I can work on three different play/fiction tasks. Stop wasting time and stop the self-pity, he said.

I didn't want to turn my attention to this other play that's halfway written, but Peter said: hurry up, I'm here for a limited time, not for eternity. But he's been very reassuring about a lot of small details in my life. We've had a lot of arguments because I'm not used to anybody giving me orders...but it's been good.

The novel: He wants you to read *The New Yorker* article on crime fiction, April 9.07, pg. 91, just arrived in the mail this week. It's about crime fiction not taking itself too seriously. Check out its tips on style, he's saying. Peter chuckled as I read it the other morning. I tried to get through Don DeLillo's short story in the same issue, but it was too full of itself (Peter agreed.)

Peter's spirit has been very happy with animals, birds twittering a lot when I go out in the morning, a skunk, cats, a poodle jumping on me. He also said animal souls or whatever are in the great space very conspicuously.

Today I was doing my grocery shopping in Chinatown, and when I picked up a bunch of broccoli, a big brown spider bit me, a first. Wow! It was painful. Peter thought it was hilarious. And he said: you're in for a lot of firsts.

Another friend of mine commented about Peter: don't let this overwhelm you.

And Peter said I'm in the driver's seat with this. My neighbor got a new hybrid Toyota, and when I pulled up next to it in the garage, I realized Peter was in it, having fun with the controls and even the new car smell??!! I think it was his way of reinforcing that I'm in the driver's seat.

I've kind of learned how to handle this whole thing on my own terms because he's a patient kind of spirit. Whatever I can't take in, Peter waits and says it quietly when I'm calmed down.

I'm happy Peter came in your dream.

again, much love, Faith

> *You've been having whopping orgasms these past*
> *couple of days*
> *Peter, this doesn't feel moral. Your wife is grieving.*
> *You have a passionate friendship with your self*
> *I like that*

April 5, 2007

Alexis,

Wow! My dad loved animals too. He absolutely loved them. My mother said he wanted to be a veterinarian in college, but was not allowed to major in animal science. They both went to a historically-black college, Langston Univ. in Oklahoma.

My dad was a big gambler and loved the race track...he taught my brother handicapping from going to see the horses—that's where my brother saw Dad's love of the horses, not just the gambling.

When all of this started, I got a picture of a dog with a badly mangled face, like it had been in a car accident, and Peter immediately said: don't worry, there are plenty of dogs and animals here. What you're seeing is not scary.

My father and sis were dog people and my big brother loves his cat. We all got very attached to each pet. Had elaborate funerals for them as kids.

Peter really likes Oakland. He said if he had known it was this nice, he might have lived here. Peter said he got tired of the driving hassle in LA He likes that I can zip around in Oakland and get anywhere in 10 minutes. Peter adds: and I do zip around.

Peter says: *this could be a much better experience if you'd really settle into it, you block me so much. And he says: you could really help Alexis with C.*

I was looking at Oprah today and at one point I cleared off one of the sofas for Peter, which he'd asked me to do a while ago. We settled into a show on autism, and he kept saying that it reminded him of C.

So at one point, Oprah did her usual commentary, and I said, "Oh, she kills me. She's so self-satisfied." And during the commercial break, Peter said: *You're like that. You're good at what you're good at...but, for instance, you need to listen to Marta more carefully.*

Marta is so longwinded. He said: *No, she's pouring out her heart to you, and you're thinking, Marta, you're covering the same stuff from yesterday. But she's not exactly.*

Marta always asks about Peter too, and she performed the sage burning ceremony that first week when I was frightened in my sleep. Today Marta said she was glad I'm welcoming Peter better now.

Oh, today—when I carried up my groceries, I had to go up and down the two flights about six times. Peter said: *I wish I could help you.* I was so touched. I said: please, don't do any of that stuff like in the movies, as in: I'm going to find you a nice guy. All my friends know I hate them to do matchmaking for me.

When I was putting the food up and when I was shopping for it, he said: *it's about time you got some food in the refrigerator.*

He's right: I could enjoy this more if I let myself. But I'm wary. Just me. Peter said: *you know you're basically a distrustful person. You don't trust people enough to let them into your heart. That's why you don't have a guy.* This is a trip—a stone gas.

my love, Faith

You have no ego

Your ego is all about warmth
For you, warmth is ego
That's why you devour food
Fuel—you're trying to get warm
Also you're not afraid of death
You're very close to it
Always have been with the nightmares, the day-
dreaming
You keep crossing back and forth
going from hot to cold trying to get warm
That's why you like sarcastic men
Sarcasm is warmth for the brain
Angry men, you love angry men
They heat it up

April 5, 2007

Alexis,

I've been thinking about what Peter said: *this is the core of what's held me back as a writer, the unwillingness to confront the sadness. If you're sad, you're sad. You have the ability to write funny. That's great. That's rare. But you also have the eye to see human suffering and you tend to stay away from it. Confront it. It won't kill you.*

I have this quote from decades ago, Maeterlinck: Your thoughts irradiate from you as from a transparent vase. I've tried to conceal mine. Peter has pressed me to share my son's story with you.

A few years ago, my son got in big trouble. I got him and my ex, who didn't want to talk at that point, talking. My son, college-educated, intelligent, cleaned up his act and has a good position now. But it was an ordeal and I had to stay calm throughout because, as you know, cooler heads must prevail.

When kids mess up after you've raised them and they've gone out into the world, it's such heartache. But I contend it's spiritual. When my son was having his problems, I wanted him to surface from them with some wisdom, a greater humanity.

Some people have to hit the bottom before they can come up and learn one of life's harsh lessons—you can't get your happiness at other people's expense.

Anyway, Peter has been bugging me to tell you this.

my love again, Faith

April 7, 2007

Alexis, this was the letter I wrote to my son in the middle of his ordeal.

Hang in there, hon. Often people want to help with grief but are at a loss as to what to do. Let girlfriends and guy friends help you out with the celebrations — totally. Parcel it out. Otherwise it won't be a celebration for you. It'll just be that day you were wiped out.

love, Faith

> My dear son,
>
> We don't get to talk so much anymore. So I needed to write and let you know how I as a mom and a grandmother feel. I have strong confidence that, in spite of the problems you're going through, you're going to pull through and push forward. This is a great test of your maturity. It may last longer than you want, but when it passes you'll be a different man.
>
> A child, let alone a son that's your spitting image, is a great gift. You have a right, an obligation and the privilege to parent him. His mom is a force of nature, unstoppable, and that is the meaning of mother. Mothers do what we do by instinct *as well as* by training. Your great fortune is her love for this kid you two brought in this world. It can turn into your great misfortune if you let that overshadow *your* parenting.
>
> I enjoy his being a fortunate kid. But he needs to know that "to him whom much is given, will much be required." That's something you can teach him in many different ways, by playing with him, talking with him, reading him children's books, giving him chunks of your time. Otherwise, he will grow into a monster. Very simply a monster, a person who expects everything and gives nothing. Because mothers, women, are givers by nature.
>
> It is past time for you to step up and be a full-scale father. One mistake I see that black men make with their kids is letting the mothers do it all. One mistake I see that black parents make with their kids is thinking the schools should do it all. No, that's not the way it is. Parents have to mold their kids.
>
> Dear, that's your job in life: to raise this kid. Whatever you do to earn a living legally is what you do to make

money. Don't let the hassles of life—which **never** go away—get in front of your parenting. You waited 32 years to become a parent. Now you're a dad for the rest of your life. He is watching everything you do, and he adores you.

I still expect my Mother's Day present: for you to spend **30 days straight** seeing him every day. I love you, son. You got the son you wanted. You have as much right as his mother to parent him. I don't care if she has more money, her own house, a better job, better credit. Maybe she'll always have more marbles. Have you thought of that? If you don't have but a can of beans, give him what you can and love and surround him. That's parenting. **It's not how much you give materially; it's how much you give of yourself.** Nobody can take away all the nights and days we played acey-deucy, Monopoly and Scrabble, the walking through the snow to go to Friendly's for ice-cream sundaes. Nobody can subtract my presence in your childhood from your life.

I can never compete with your dad's family for all they've done for you. Sometimes I get jealous and know you are ashamed of what I offer materially. But it doesn't matter. Not a bit. I did my best and am proud of that. I was **intensely** ashamed of my parents' house as a young person. Why didn't they keep it up? Why wasn't it nicer? Why? Why? Why? It took me into my 30s and to start chanting before I could appreciate that they were individuals and not just my parents. I forgave them; one of my two noble deeds has been helping Dad die; the other was letting you go to live in California with your dad.

Just before you left, you asked if you could be honest with me. You said you didn't want to end up where I was at 37 when you got to be 37. That was profound. Well, you're almost 37. I wouldn't wish my struggle as an artist/writer/teacher on anyone. But I am proud that I spent my 20s and 30s raising a fine son. I don't regret for a minute any of the sacrifices and time I spent making sure you came up right. You can't just *tell* your kid, you have to lead by example. And you can only do that by spending time with him constantly.

Life is good. In fact, life is beautiful whether you have a lot or a little. With wisdom, you'll see that.

love, Mom

April 9, 2007

Hi Alexis,

Peter has had me working my tail off. He has become like a personal trainer inside my head, focusing on my daily discipline and on not getting discouraged when I get rejections. He kept telling me, move that bike, move the bike. My bike was in front of my writing files for the winter, and I didn't realize it was blocking me from getting to writing tasks. But Peter knew. I was getting irritated at his insistence but finally got to it.

Whoa! The things I found, including the flyer from the play that I worked on with Peter, going back 21 years! I put a bucket of papers into the recycle bin. Again, another instance where he said: papers, records, manuscripts. I'm not just talking about Alexis, this is advice for you.

I went to tea and lively conversation with Joyce & friends yesterday. And Peter was right there. He digs Joyce. When Joyce told our other friend who is bull-headed that she could see right through her and added, "You can't shit the shitter," Peter just went nuts. Bananas! I told Joyce, and she is as taken with Peter as he is with her.

This continues to be an amazing experience. I'm just trying to understand it. Take care.

love, Faith

April 9, 2007

Oh, thank you, Alexis, for reading *Theodicy* and, gasp, taking notes on it! I would love to get your feedback, notes, technical and otherwise. Peter speaks very highly of your indispensable role in his life as a writer…often while commenting on my lack of such a partner. We had a "thought conversation" about his good fortune in being in residence at The Rep. I shared that before he died Arthur Miller said he regretted not having an artistic home and that his output might have been way more if he had.

Theodicy has had an interesting ten months of existence. When I finished it last May, I started on revisions. Had a living room reading for my birthday, a reading in SF last fall, and then the second one with a director and staging this Feb. also in SF. No production yet, but several companies have asked to see more than the first 10 pages.

A set designer whose wife acted in both readings said he was fascinated by the technical demands, especially the river of death. About four years ago at San Jose Repertory I saw Lynn Redgrave in a play she wrote about her mother Rachel Kempson's marriage to a homosexual. There was a stream onstage made up of something like rippling stainless steel...don't know what it was for sure, but I was intrigued. The image stayed with me.

I welcome your comments.

with love, Faith

April 10, 2007

Alexis,

I like talking to you very much. Every time we speak, my view of this experience changes. You demystify Peter for me.

A few days ago, I got a rejection from Sundance. I had asked Peter the morning before: am I going to get in? Silence, then: *No...but that's nothing compared to the things that are going to develop for you.* Then he went into how Sundance ain't all that. Kind of like, stop being fooled by all the smoke and mirrors.

So I got the rejection letter and handled it well for a couple of hours, then really cried and raged and said not-nice things. He was silent, but stood right by my side as I worked on scenes, the novel, submissions the rest of Saturday night, then from Sunday afternoon on through till Monday morning at 5am. I apologized to him and thanked him.

When I said I was sorry, Peter said: *I have feelings too.*

I said: but you're dead!

Peter: *That doesn't make any difference. I felt bad.*

So I agreed to have manners with him and to learn how to handle rejection better.

Later, Peter said: *I'm not a god. I'm not a devil. I'm Peter.*

I've been working on cleaning up papers, my idea files, all these book and play ideas. When I awake in the morning, often I wait for Peter's voice to come to me. Often, as I said in our call, he gives me a word, sometimes more.

Peter said: *you don't need to make a book out of everything.*

He was talking about all my journals, notes, idea files. He said by telling myself all these years, This would make a book, This is a play idea, I have given myself too many goals to reach and a lot of frustration and disappointment in myself. Instead, he said: *regard it as your warehouse, use bits and pieces in a few plays, a book. Accept that you're not going to use everything.* This is freeing; this helped me throw away a lot of stuff.

I guess I'm much more closed—Cancer the crab—than I realized. I haven't let anyone in. It's been relatively easy to stay closed because I have lots of personality and sparkle. But that's like the humor. It only goes so far.

thank you for listening.

love, Faith

April 14, 2007

Alexis,

I'm sorry we didn't get to talk. Today was kind of sad for me too; I thought Peter had gone.

After the 40 hours of wide-awake writing on Sunday and Monday, I was so tired. After that I noticed that I only heard Peter when I was despondent or doing something impractical. Then I'd hear his voice very clearly.

As I shopped, I was aware of Peter's presence. I told him that I appreciated all he has done for me. I've really seen that I have to work on my confidence in order to write with less frenzy and more daily discipline.

When I thought Peter was gone I had a major realization: that a person's spirit is much bigger than his life...that, as you said early on, I'll always be able to call upon Peter's spirit. And that a person's spirit reaches across time, space, class, and race. I read philosophers a lot, and their spirit to challenge life's mysteries always endears me to them—and some of them lived centuries ago!

I finally understood why our plays were so alike, that Peter's spirit is a universal vibration and that I picked up on it with my play. Not to get Berkeley-corny on you, but it's been a thoughtful three or four days.

much love, Faith

Confidence
You need to have more
You need to network with your black friends
Like that's ever got me anywhere.
You need to push more
Me?
Yes, you
It's sad
I'm not a white male.
This is sad
So, I'll just be sad.

April 23, 2007

Hi Alexis,

I love the pix on the e-vite. Just wanted you to know that I've been reading aloud the responses on the invite and Peter loves hearing about who's coming...and corrects my pronunciation of their names. He also corrects everyone who says, Peter was a warm... to **is** a warm and...making me laugh so much on that account.

Also I began reading right away *We Are Their Heaven* by Allison DuBois. Very helpful and encouraging. Many sentences stop me dead in my tracks because they're so connected to not only this experience but many others I've had.

Peter at one point said: *you're not afraid of death, you're very close to death.* And that I go back and forth across the border between life and death, and that's why I have had such problems with body temperature control all my life.

I've always read obits, and lost myself in them, in the person's life. I lose myself in literature in the same way, particularly bios/autobiographies and historical fiction. I chalk it up to imagination.

DuBois says: Those who have died just want us to acknowledge that we know that they're still here. If I feel tension or irritation from the experience, it's for that reason. Once they're acknowledged, they relax, and I won't get such a feeling of urgency.

I feel that very strongly with Peter, that he needed me to acknowledge his presence and helpfulness to me and to others. So I have been doing that more and more. In my Thursday class, I talked about Peter. Almost everyone got it and loved it. I could feel Peter beaming. One said she had had the same experience with a friend who died young a month after having leukemia diagnosed. Only this friend was very miserable, had led an unsatisfying life, and her experience with her friend's spirit has been very sad, unlike mine. I reflected on how Peter's life was so successful, both in his career and personally. One student remarked, "That explains why you've been glowing." Peter just loved it, loved it.

He also said that I had not made a mistake by teaching all this time and not being a fulltime writer. Peter said I needed to grow in compassion and experience using my compassion. That is comforting. He praised me as a teacher and totally got that I teach intuitively, not by the book. That class is full of students with GEDs, all natural rebels. He also praised my speaking at a Buddhist meeting, as I went through some historical info for people. Peter said I was awesome.

Alexis, "The Loneliness of the Long Distance Runner." And "The Heart is a Lonely Hunter" — themes in my life.

He has encouraged me on finding a suitable mate. He reminded me of Ray in a dream. I loved Ray to death but he was 13 years younger. Peter said: Ray was a good guy. He's trying to get me to think outside the box on possible mates.

I love Mexican food, especially enchiladas. Peter, my mentor-in-residence and finance advisor, helped me make them myself. He said: *You can do this yourself and save mucho dinero.* So I got the fixings and made them all last week. I had tried before but they didn't come out right. I mixed in tofu which I love to include in my diet, and it was delicious...he enjoyed the meals as much as I did. He also loved watching *The Sopranos* with me. DuBois again:

...sometimes spirits will appear back here when they are needed for intervention to save the life of a living person or to help shape a person into who she was meant to be by attempting to guide that person down the right path. Usually this will be a person who reminds them of themselves and whom they want to keep from walking down the wrong path — often the path that the deceased themselves had traveled...

I also feel this very strongly with Peter. I think I told you that I had contemplated checking out before, like, who gives a damn. And I have a special relationship to trains, a love/fear. I usually have something with trains in my plays. So a couple of weeks ago, I thanked Peter for coming into my life when I really had been so despondent.

And then I went to the dr.'s which is close to a RR track. As I stood there and marveled at this great invention of the train, I felt Peter's presence and thanked him for helping me not feel alone and desolate. The lure of the other side can be strong in my life, and I needed to get a clearer understanding of life and death in this experience.

love, Faith

April 23, 2007

Wow, Alexis,

This just keeps developing. I had noticed that I feel much more comfortable cooking and baking from scratch—waffles, scrambled eggs w/cheese, a whole chicken—at home. Last night I did shrimp with rotini and curry.

And I'm throwing out less food...all since the beginning of the year. Also I made oatmeal-raisin-pineapple cookies and I could feel Peter saying yummy.

Yes, Friday night is good for me. I gave my Saturday class May 12th as a go-see-a-play day. So that's taken care of. Thank you so much.

I understand your time demands. Take care. I'm thinking of you.

love, Faith

April 23, 2007

Alexis,

Just one thing that keeps happening—black cats keep stopping or staring at me, or walking away from me, not crossing my path. There's a black cat on the way to Marta's where I go daily to chant at 7am. At first it was crossing my path. Now it knows I'm coming and starts ahead of me, looking back, as if to say, "I'm getting out of your way, sister."

On a hilly street I drove down today, a black cat stared me down but didn't move. Dogs too keep coming up to me, one owner saying, "Oh don't be scared. This dog is a Casanova. I can't keep him away from the ladies." Peter just cracks up.

Get your rest, get your down time, and don't forget to take that hour just for you.

love, Faith

April 24, 2007

Hi Alexis,

I know you're busy, busy. I'm just sending this newest *Theodicy* on because I did almost everything you suggested. Thank you very much. It all helped clarify the play even more.

Please don't run yourself ragged. Peter said: *don't let the cat have kittens over this. Motor down??!!*

I'm off to the hospital, seems I have a detached retina. Of all things.

My dad would say: take it easy, squeezie.

with love, Faith

April 25, 2007

Alexis,

Just got back from the hospital at 4:15am. They ran all kinds of tests and say it's a detached retina but in the back of my eye, a less dangerous position. So it's all right for me to see an ophthalmologist (shades of Oba in *Theodicy*!) next Wednesday.

I had been having flashes of light out of my right eye whenever I turned my head, for about two weeks. I thought it was connected to Peter.

Then early last week I started seeing like double refractions of light and curves and even box shapes out of the same eye. I went on the Internet and it seemed to match retinal detachment. The advice: go to yr dr. immediately. It could result in loss of an eye. So after much prodding from u-no-hoo, I went yesterday.

The FAQs say it comes with middle age or later often, or blunt trauma or diabetes. No blunt trauma. My family has diabetes on both sides, but they tested my blood sugar tonight. It's still normal. As is eye pressure. And blood pressure for which I take meds.

Thank you so much for your concern. And for the good word to T.

Peter said about me getting the revision done yesterday and this eye stuff: *You really have to be driven by the threat, imaginary or otherwise, of death to get your work out, don't you?*

We argued about my going to the hospital. I went at 2pm to county general and couldn't sit hours and wait another two hrs just to be registered. So I came home and finished my work on the play, then went back.

much love, Faith

Alexis said she's trying to recall if you had a detached retina from softball

---

April 29, 2007

Hi Alexis,

I hope you are feeling good. You should be. You are a wonderful person and were partner to a wonderful person. This experience gets deeper and deeper.

Peter said: *somebody named Rene is going to be very inquisitive about all of this, especially at the memorial.* Peter is looking forward very much to it. He said Marisa or Melissa is feeling very saddened by his death. He can see her weeping. This tears him up too.

Peter said he is trying to pry open my heart. He said, *wow, that's a big job.* He has me trying to understand compassion from the inside out. He says I understand it with my head, not so much with my heart. I am always worried about getting damaged.

Alexis, I viewed the psychic on TV for the first time this week. Peter said: *you can learn something from her. You think you have to be right. All you have to be is encouraging and say what you see and hear.*

I don't want to be a psychic, I just want to be Faith. But Peter says: *You have to be what you are, not this projected image.* Alexis, a lot's going on.

much love from me to you, Faith

April 29, 2007

Alexis,

You're right. I know it, about being psychic; I guess I'm just kinda ashamed of my gift, and don't like being ostracized because of it. Geez, I have so much growing to do.

By now, I think you know we are very much alike. And that's comforting. And I do appreciate the solace I've been able to give you.

I read this bio of FDR, one of my favorite people. And it said when his mother, the matriarch of the family, died, a huge oak tree toppled in the back of her home. Something like that. I read it ages ago. But my point is that Peter's passing is like that. A big event.

A few weeks ago, I was frightened of Peter because he said: *why don't you join me?* I thought he was advocating suicide. So I stupidly tried to do one of Marta's sage-burning ceremonies and told Peter to leave. There was smoke in every room of my apt., I went to bed coughing (laughable now), and woke up next morning with Peter standing there saying: *Look at this. You filled your whole house with smoke and you're not even a smoker, and I'm still here!!* I told Marta, and she said, Faith, you're supposed to open your windows! Duh!

It's taken me a while to process all this, reading Allison DuBois, and being quiet and listening, all to understand that Peter keeps trying to open me up to what I've been doing all my life, crossing back and forth, walking with spirits, having an active dream life. Throughout my 30s, when I met Peter, I had a hyper-dream life that started when my head hit the pillow.

Anyway, shortly after filling my room with smoke, my ex-father-in-law came to me in a dream and told me some important things which I relayed to my ex-hubby and his wife about our son and grandson.

still here, still trying, Faith

210

May 3, 2007

Hi Alexis,

I've had you on my mind off and on the last couple of days.
Hope all is well and the preparations for Peter's memorial
aren't too taxing. I would think they are.

I spent 5-1/2 hrs. at the hospital eye clinic yesterday to finally
hear that I don't have a detached retina, but do have a detached
vitreous lens. Not as serious, but the dr. said I did the right
thing by coming to emergency. There is no treatment. It happens with aging. They said I'll get used to those spots, and if
many more appear ("like a swarm of bees") then it would mean
retinal detachment or tear and to come in to emergency.

So here's to no surgery. Hallelujah.

love, Faith

> I don't want to go to the celebration.
> I don't have any money to go.
>> Alexis is paying for everything
> I can't have her do that.
> And my car caught on fire.
>> You're trying every which way you can not to go
> I'm gonna feel awkward and out of place.
> I'm not LA or Hollywood.
>> So what?

May 6, 2007

Alexis, Is my e-mail from March 19th cool for the celebration?
I played down the mystic aspect. I can always write something
else—no problem.

love, Faith

> I can't believe I went to your thing, your memorial.
>
> Meeting Alexis was wonderful. She accepted me fully. I felt
> like a member of the family. Your oldest son looks just like
> you. I thought Alexis would want me to downplay the mystic
> stuff when I spoke.
>
> And being black, too, I thought I was going to be so out of
> place. I was prepared to be uncomfortable. But it was the
> total opposite. Of course you had black friends and peers.
> Your plays all had black people in them

Ah, your issue with trust
It felt like the dream where the sun was shining brilliantly
and you were smiling at me. Why didn't you tell me you
were visiting others?
Not necessary
Six people including me testified about their mystical
experiences with you. I was utterly transfixed by all the tes-
timonials. Three hours worth! I loved when you got your first
big check from the studio.

Your friend said the two of you stood on the mountain and
pissed all over Hollywood

I felt you there all afternoon.
And this was just LA
Wait till New York

The composer guy sitting next to me was so nervous going
over his notes. I was blown away when he got up. He said
you stood over his shoulder for three days straight. Pushing
him to finish his libretto. Exactly like you stayed by my side
for the 40 hours it took to finish the play. I can't believe it.
You're a fucking ghost.
A good one
I thought I would be creeped out when Alexis took me
upstairs to your studio. I really didn't want to go there. I
thought the two worlds would collide.

Living Peter, dead Peter
You're a scaredy-cat
But as soon as I walked up the stairs, I instantly knew
you. All the pictures of your productions and you with the
stars in your movies. My favorite part was your son telling
how he was five when your father died. He came to you in
the kitchen and said that grandpa had told him something.
You asked him where he heard grandpa say that. And he
said in the dining room, grandpa's in the dining room.

And you told him, go tell grandpa to get the hell back where
he came from.
Biggest laugh of the afternoon
Thanks for pushing me to go.
I'm good to go
Good to go

May 14, 2007

Alexis, Alexis,

What a weekend. I was moved to tears so much. I was very happy for you that it all came off...not just came off but it came off beautifully...a great tribute to Peter, to your inspiring marriage and life together and for his children and all of us who were nurtured by Peter.

Now I understand clearly Peter's presence these last months. This was the tribe he was talking about. I felt it 100%. All my questions got answered, speech by speech, conversation by conversation, moment by moment.

I sat next to the composer from The Rep. When he finished talking and sat down, I put my hand on his trembling arm and said, "We had the same experience." We were the waterworks twins during the whole thing. It was so gratifying to hear so many acknowledge Peter's continuing presence. I had to laugh. What power.

You've perhaps been seeing this for a while. But I have to say I was very moved by Peter's kids, who seemed to be taking on Peter's legacy in front of us all. What a responsibility. What a mission.

I could not get to bed until 4am this morning. But as soon as my head hit the pillow, the tears flowed like a river. And they were tears of joy, tears of love. Like Peter told me, love, yeah, there's erotic love and romantic love, but there's also the love of compassion and connectedness. That's what I felt from the moment I saw you in the parking lot and you were motioning for me to get in the car.

Thank you so much for welcoming me into this circle. You are a powerhouse of a woman. I can't express how deeply I feel about you. It was absolutely necessary for me to be there. Thanks to you and to Peter for pushing me to leave my comfort zone. I found a great circle.

much love, Faith

May 15, 2007

Alexis,

Found this quote in today's NY Times:

"People always think I must be so tough to survive all this. But I'm a real softie. But maybe that's what it takes — you have to be soft to survive. Hard people shatter."

–Kate Webb, war correspondent

I love this!

Hope you're getting lots of rest. I am. The weekend was like a Jack LaLanne workout in Joy.

Peter is as busy as ever here. He is so pleased that I got 100% verification from the celebration that he's a real presence in my own and others' lives. Peter says: I feel really acknowledged, proud and grateful that all those people had a good time at my expense.

He keeps rubbing his hands together and saying, *Faith, let's get down to business now, as a writer.*

Alexis, Peter said he loved the celebration and thanks you for hanging in there. Things are going to improve tremendously—you're due a big upper—and you're going to feel like putting on a floppy hat and strutting around very soon. Peter said when it occurs, please don't feel guilty about it. Have fun. This one's on him.

much love, get well, Faith

May 21, 2007

Hi Alexis,

Hope all is well. I've been so at ease with all of this since the celebration of life.

I know that Peter is feeling well-acknowledged. And relaxed. Marta asked how I felt about it all now. I feel Peter as much but it's far more comforting.

I left the *Theodicy* manuscript on your desk, top center, in a large white envelope...and Saturday was my last day of school. So I get a couple of weeks until summer session. I'm determined to clear up clutter and finish my spring cleaning.

much love, Faith

May 22, 2007

Alexis,

So glad to hear from you. I wondered, then hoped you weren't sad after all the celebrating. You wrote: I had a chat with him this morning but...it was a one way chat.

So many of my chats with Peter are one-way at first. Then he speaks up later in the day, or in the week, or in a dream. One thing I've noticed is that Peter as a presence likes action. As long as I'm resting or chilling, he's not here so much. But let me get in a jam, or get to walking, or on that freeway he's right there...he loves going. And helping.

This morning, I did my laundry and accidentally locked my keys in the building laundry room. I sat on the terrace waiting for someone to come along and then Peter said: *What are you going to do, big mamma? We can't sit here all day. We have things to do.* I had to get to SF to my dental apt.

So I knocked on my downstairs neighbor's door and used his key to open the laundry room. Peter said: *this is your problem. You won't take immediate action.*

Also before my car caught on fire, I had a humongous dream in which I thought Peter was leaving for good. This is because I thought I was awake and saw Peter leave in a big ball of fire and dust and drama out the window...it was so amazing that it took so much of his energy to leave, to burst out of the fireball and burst out of the window. He had his head down pushing hard like an athlete going for the goal.

Then I woke up and realized it was a dream and not happening in my conscious state. During the dream, I was dumbfounded. When I awoke, tears streamed down my face. I thought it was a mystic leave-taking or something. I thought it was Peter's way of leaving.

So it wasn't until after the car stuff had calmed down that I remembered the dream. And then Peter came back and said: *I was trying to warn you that your car was catching fire. It was an internal fire that was caused by faulty wiring.*

He keeps saying, *you can't get rid of me that easily.*

So, Alexis, I guess there's still work to be done. Also Peter said: *this all would be a very good sitcom but on the order of* Curb Your Enthusiasm, *a wicked updating of* Bewitched.

much love, again and again, Faith

May 24, 2007

Alexis,

I got the title of the show/play/sitcom and the underlying theme and conflict all in one: *Acknowledge Me!*

Here's the guy's dilemma...let's call him Dixon: He was an acclaimed and successful writer, lover of the good life, much loved, respected, a man who had a great life, looked younger than his years, a great raconteur, and a ladies' man in his day.

In death, almost no one recognizes that he's still around, close to all his loved ones, his many students and protégés, wanting to help and aid them. They can't hear, see, touch or feel him.

Except for this former student of his who has this untapped intuitive gift which she realizes when he takes up residence in her one-bedroom apt. in another city...**and** his dogs and his cat. Let's call her Faith.

Most of all, his loving wife, Hope, is drowning in sorrow, just the opposite of what he would have wanted. In death, he has to bust his butt to get her attention. He says: *this is as hard as writing.*

Acknowledge Me!
Ghost meets *Bewitched*

Other characters:

- His oldest son, who feels the burden of the legacy of a great father. And perhaps translates it as unbridled ambition and cocksmanship.

- Faith's circle of eccentric friends including:

    🖐 Aviva, her masseuse/intuitive who senses Dixon right away,

    🖐 Marta, a Native-American/Latina who welcomes Dixon but whose boyfriend is jealous of Dixon,

    🖐 Joyce whose late grandmother, big Momma, hangs out with Dixon in The Great Space.

Alexis, just add your thoughts/notes/characters/real people with fake names to these and we'll get enough in a bit to start writing.

xoxo, Faith

216

May 25, 2007

Alexis,

I forgot this: About the time of Peter's birthday, May 3, he started bugging me.

"Bake me a cake for my birthday."

And I kept saying, Peter, I can't have a whole cake in the house. My sweet tooth would go crazy.

He insisted: *I want you to bake a cake for my birthday.* He drove me nuts about this.

Well, I was in the hospital for the 5-1/2 hour visit on May 2, and he was so pleased that nothing drastic was wrong with my eyes. He said: *So now I get my cake.*

The next day, I was at the dentist who was repairing my cracked molar. And I had to give a test that night at school. Even so he insisted.

I said: Peter, you're carrying on.

And he said: *I'm used to arguing on my birthday*
(???!!!)

A couple of nights later he just argued me into taking a candle, putting it into an iced cinnamon bun that I had, lighting it, turning out all the lights and singing happy birthday to him, a la Marilyn Monroe to JFK style.

That pleased him and I ate the roll and went to bed.

Peter is a total trip.

my love, Faith

> *Alexis said you did the cinnamon bun thing with her.*
> *You're a glutton.*
> > *I keep telling you: don't tell her everything.*

May 28, 2007

Alexis,

Yeah, you're on the money. I was painting in broad strokes to get a sense of the conflict, the tension. In reality, my great realization was coming to the celebration of life and hearing so many at the memorial talk about their closeness to Peter after death. That reassured me that I wasn't daffy, and in the script sense, it can always come in as a device that Faith feels isolated and goofy at the intrusiveness of the spirit. Yet she always finds out or the audience always sees how others too are seeing/feeling/hearing/smelling Peter.

You're right. One thing we want to work out is Who sees him and when and how and....One interesting device, instead of "They can't hear, see, touch or feel him…" might be that one person can see him, another can smell the cigar, yet another says, "That's Peter touching my arm. He was tactile." While others hear his voice. But maybe the two primary characters, the Alexis and the Faith characters, keep getting multiple manifestations of him…Just ideas.

I have collaborated a lot, most notably with the play I co-wrote for the SF Mime Troupe, "Knocked Up," a commedia dell'arte about a girl who gets pregnant and the village won't let her abort. So a comet goes over the town and mysteriously all the men get pregnant, morning sickness, big bellies, and have to get gynecological exams. Finally they get so exasperated, they let her take the RU486 pill. But the twist at the end: her boyfriend decides he wants to stay pregnant and have the baby himself. Big laughs, big bawdy fun.

Also, I was thinking the title has so many shadings to it. Peter wants to be acknowledged in death as he was in life, yet the two women want to acknowledge themselves (maybe both having caretaker fatigue in one way or another, and just being women who care for others intensely). And others need to be acknowledged—the family, friends, the dogs, etc. Again, ideas.

I'm grateful about Peter's role in bringing us to each other.

Love, Faith

May 28, 2007

Alexis,

I had a good time at this bbq that I almost didn't go to, lots of lively discussion and good eats. So necessary to join the living.

Tomorrow I want you, please, please, please, to get up, shower or bathe, put on deodorant, go to your _____ *
and meet and greet FOR AT LEAST TWENTY MINUTES. Time it. Talk with somebody outside of your home. You have to prepare for New York by getting out and about a little bit every day...otherwise you'll be bombarded by NY and the days after will be hell. NY is an assault on the senses of a normal aggressive person, let alone if you're vulnerable.

* favorite shop, bookstore or library, gym, craft place, etc.

Other ideas came up while I was walking to the bbq. Mind you, all ideas, not wedded to any of them:

- Faith has trouble going to sleep at night
- Alexis has trouble getting out of the house
- Faith walks for exercise, up and down the small hills of her neighborhood, huffing and puffing
- Alexis walks her dogs
- Faith finds out in the NY Times that Peter has died
- Alexis finds Faith's tribute to Peter on the internet and writes her a brief note.
- Faith replies
- They start an internet exchange, remembering Peter
- He begins to stride along with each on the walks
- This could be the time when he spouts stuff about writing to Faith, and about keeping his papers, letters, manuscripts to Alexis
- Some of the episodes with songs between Alexis and Peter could come in as flashbacks when she's missing him

Our talk today helped me **see** a story. I'm a visualizer.

I think we're on our way.

love and affection, Faith

May 30, 2007

We must remember to check in while we're coming up with ideas.

Alexis,

I totally agree. When I don't hear from you, I start thinking, did I upset her? Is she sinking into sorrow? So we need to keep up a rhythm of communication. I've attached a general scheme for the story. Again, nothing set in stone, but, boy oh boy, do we have a lot of stuff.

I've been working at my p/t job where I score essays for all kinds of tests like GMAT, GRE, and SAT. I'm telling you we can learn from Glenn, one of my co-workers.

Glenn is about as narcissistic as they come. He was scoring next to me today, and he runs through his stacks of essays like a bull in Pamplona, and then props up his New Yorker and reads it page by page all day. Screw the job, he wants to read his New Yorker.

219

Glad to hear that you are *thinking* about being narcissistic and selfish. And also glad to hear that you're seeing some light at the end of the tunnel. Keep going.

love you, Faith

June 4, 2007

Alexis,

I have been so pooped from scoring essays that I just come in, flop, get up a while later, check on everything and flop again. So I didn't worry. I was dead sleep as soon as I sent off the e-mail. I too had been thinking of you.

—gotta go scour my sink and get to bed as early as I can.

love you, be well, Faith

June 9, 2007

Hi Alexis,

Hope you're well in the process of getting ready for NY. It's pretty exciting. Isn't it like the other half of the equation... the celebration of life?

I'm working slower but deeper on *Acknowledge Me*. The theme of friendship is, I have come to realize, *passionate friendship*; the many conversations Peter and I have had are full of intensity, argument, lots of back and forth.

This whole episode in my life has caused me to do a lot of soul searching. To explain it to myself. To make it a part of my whole life. To understand its mystic component. And, always, to ponder the question, why me?

love you much, Faith

Here's some scenes/dialogue that Faith has with Peter. Still working on the scenes we set up, but had to set (or perhaps find) a tone:

(Faith is driving down the highway, in the countryside. Peter, sitting in the passenger seat, begins to hum along with the music on her radio)

Faith: Why?

Peter: Why what?

Faith: Why are you here?

He smiles.

Faith: Why me? And don't do that simplistic why-not-you stuff?

(They go further down the road)

Faith: Why me? I took one course with you for ten weeks ages ago...And I'm black and you're white. Why would you come into my life?

Why?

Why?

What does it serve you? And what does it serve me?

(They drive on for a while in silence. Peter has an enigmatic smile.)

Peter: I love you.

(Faith nearly loses control of the car.)

Peter: Whoa!

(Faith regains control of the car. Again, silence.)

Peter: I always have; I always will.

(Sade's "this is no ordinary love" plays. Peter smiles. Faith looks at him smiling.)

Peter: (motions to the road) Don't lose control again. You're among the living.

(Here, at the intercutting, scene with Alex needs to show the intensity/eroticism/sexuality of the marriage.)

July 6, 2007

Alexis,

Oh yeah, oh yeah. Good to be back in contact with you, Alexis. You are good for me.

Responding to Peter's visits, my Nigerian friend threw his hands across his ears and said: "I don't want to know about anything I can't see or touch or hear...That's what destroyed Africa—superstition." That was his frame of reference.

My friend who grew up Jehovah's Witness said each person reacts to this kind of spiritual experience according to the way they were brought up. At first she thought, "Ah, it's a demon!" because that's what her religion taught her as a kid. Once she listened to me, she recognized that it was joyful and comforting to me.

I totally understand you're busy right now. My hands are pretty full too.

Take care, go to bed early, get up and lace up those shoes, girl!

My best and love, Faith

> *I saved this article from the newspaper, Peter.*
> > *I was wondering when you were going to bring that up*
> *The man in the article reminded me of you.*
> > *Because he's white?*
> *No, you know what else.*
> > *Oh, that. He went up to Washington State and checked out?*
> *Euthanasia. Assisted death…is that what you did?*
> > *I wasn't going to put my family through prolonged suffering*
> *But nobody talks about it?*
> > *In polite society, it's not done*
> > *It's like discussing bathroom habits*
> *When Alexis showed me the picture in your studio the day before you died-*
> > *That was her polite way of telling you*
> *And you were standing in the meadow with your arms out-stretched. I knew.*
> > *Maybe if I had stuck around a little longer*
> *Died a little each day? Prolonged it?*
> > *Maybe Alexis' grief…*
> *My mom had Alzheimer's for a decade.*
> > *Let's not get extreme*
> > *I'm talking a fortnight*

August 12, 2007

Alexis,

I've been thinking about you for the last couple of weeks. Hope all is going well in NYC. And that you are connecting with the good people in your life.

I've had such a creative time working on my novel since summer school let out.

My spirits have been high—an agent asked to see the novel after reading an excerpt. That's given me impetus to work through this revision.

I sprint through to get as much writing done Fri-Sat-Sun since getting work at the performing arts center Mon-Thur. afternoons.

Wishing you well and a release of tension in swimming and other healthy paths.

love, Faith

Sept. 24, 2007

Alexis,

Eileen Heckart Drama for Seniors Competition 2007 Winners Announced!

Theodicy was one of 186 full-length plays submitted to the competition; my revised version, thanks-to-you-and-Peter, ended up **first runner-up**.

I feel like I'm in Atlantic City at the Miss America contest, teary-eyed, boobs propped up to my chin, hoping the winner has nude photos from the past that will surface quickly.

Alexis, thank you for giving it all a nudge. The phrase "award-winning" helps people to say, I think, subconsciously: "Oh, a committee's already read the doggone thing and certified it So there must be something to it."

I cannot thank you enough for your professional eye. It was the kick that put it in the end zone.

Onward to a full production, Faith

Alexis said I need to share this. THIS IS THE GOOD STUFF.
It's good work. You're just getting started.
It just crossed my mind that if my car went in the lake and
sunk, who would give a fuck?
Lots of people
You did it...took your own life.
I was at death's door, little girlfriend

Nov. 19, 2007

Alexis,

I still feel Peter's presence. It's actually stronger than earlier this year. It's like a guiding force in my life. I'm finding that many issues he and I touched upon in the spring are now bearing fruit. Peter insisted I had to make more connections with the prominent, well-known and bourgeois blacks that I know. And I have begun to do this, with some reluctance since I have been so anti-establishment most of my adult life.

I was asked to read poetry at a benefit for a black studies department at SFSU that I helped found 40 years ago. I did not want to go or to do it. I even swore to myself that I was too old to go. When the night came to go, last Friday, I had no excuse, got all dolled up, drove downtown and found myself the only woman on the program. What a shame if I had let my lesser ego win and stayed home...and what an honor to have been asked to read. I also met two important contacts.

Peter constantly implores me to listen more carefully to others, like Marta. I've tried to ignore his presence but it's strong and constant. He affirms that while this is a difficult period I have to move through this fog to become a successful writer. It's like he's a witness to all my internal struggles, an ally, a spiritual neighbor.

Hope all is well. I think of you often.

love, Faith

Dec. 21, 2007

Alexis,

Thank you for allowing me to be a part of this grieving process. I have learned so much. One of my puzzles about Peter was, of course, why me, why now, why didn't I know Peter later?

I met Peter when his quest for wholeness and success had some resemblance to mine right now. I thoroughly identify with Peter's, for lack of a better term, soulfulness. And I think that's the point of connection between the three of us.

Peter is definitely still around. I had a long talk about discretion with him as I was finishing the novel. So many parts of the novel derive from real life. I was always nervous about how to use what I've seen and heard as I create a fictional narrative.

Peter said always self-disclose more than I disclose about others. Isn't that interesting?

as always, much love, Faith

> *Why are you still here?*
> > *I love you*
> *That old song*
> > *I always have, I always will*
> *I can't figure out what that means*
> > *I love you!*
> *What does that mean? You're married.*
> > *Till death do us part*
> *What does it mean? You can't take me out or make love to me.*
> > *There's more than romantic love or sexual love*
> *I wasn't so good at either.*
> > *There is greater love*
> > *Involving connection and compassion*
> *I didn't know I was getting into all that. You were a fantasy lover to put myself to sleep and get over Ray*
> > *You thought your thoughts were private*
> > *What about that psychic stuff you taught people?*
> *I didn't think it extended beyond death. For me it was meta stuff between people.*
> > *You pulled me to you*

Mar. 3, 2008

Hi Alexis,

Peter's still here. I didn't want to upset you and wanted you to not grieve unnecessarily. But your guy is still around these parts. He comes and goes very quietly, but said he's been around for the hard parts, so why shouldn't he be here when my balloon goes up?

I'm writing a play with a spirit guide only I made her a woman, the younger self of the main character who gets very sick.

In writing it, I reviewed a lot of our letters. Wow, what an experience we had. Totally wonderful and very profound.

I finished my novel on Dec. 30 and an agent is reading it now.

I'm sure that Peter has helped me tremendously in many ways, not the least of which is feeling so alone.

with love and wishing you good spirits, Faith

Dec. 5, 2011

To my dear friends, writing cohorts, spiritual buddies and those whose shoulders I've cried on:

My novel sold today to Viking!!!

I'M A NOVELIST,
I'M A NOVELIST,
I'M A NOVELIST.

Faith

Praise and reviews for Judy Juanita's Virgin Soul

"Funny and wise ...a captivating tale about self-love told through the eyes of an unforgettable heroine." —Essence ☞ "Witty and deeply engaging ...about ideas and the passions generated by revolution and romantic love." —Los Angeles Times ☞ "Electrifying...Virgin Soul yields an engaging coming-of-age story, one that recalls a turbulent era in captivating prose." —San Jose Mercury News ☞ "Juanita's prose immediately immerses the reader in the time and place of its lead character...[who] progresses from middle-class 'good girl' to member of the Black Panthers, witnessing and experiencing the poverty, violence, excesses and rhetoric of the time, a transition handled by Juanita with assured matter-of-factness ...The unique perspective she offers on a volatile period of American history gives the narrative immediacy and authenticity." —Publishers Weekly ☞ "An entertaining story of a young woman's experience with one of the most radical counterculture organizations in America's history." —Bust Magazine ☞ "[With] rhythmic language and nervy dialog ...this wild ride through the rise of the militant Black Panther Party highlights differing viewpoints within the civil rights movement of the Vietnam era. Fans of Bernice McFadden will enjoy discovering this new author." —Library Journal ☞ "An intriguing look at coming-of-age in the 1960s." —Booklist ☞ "Virgin Soul is first class awesome, every page a crackling hungry flame. This novel about a young studious woman immersed in the black revolutionary experience of 60's Berkeley has a freshness and bright ardor that is rare in this lazy climate of American fiction." —Joy Williams, author of State of Grace ☞ "Hard to believe it's been almost fifty years since the formation of the Black Panthers. The novel captures that time's particular combination of violence and possibility, and the urgency of young people who invested everything in the possibility of change, even as grand rhetoric was undercut by very human failings. Geniece is smart, wounded, hopeful, and tough. It's a pleasure to grow with her through these pages." —Jean Thompson, author of The Humanity Project and The Year We Left Home ☞ "Virgin Soul is Judy Juanita's exciting debut, a coming-of-age novel set in a time of peace, love and revolution. Juanita presents a heroine, wise, naive and world-wary at eighteen who finds her voice in the Black Panthers' deadly struggle for liberation in 1960s America. Though a work of historical fiction, Virgin Soul is an intimate work, heart-breaking and compulsively readable." — Evan Wright, author of Generation Kill ☞ "A novel so unlike any I've read in years—a little of Al Young's poetry and humor, a little of Toni Cade Bambara's boldness, but Judy Juanita has given us a Bay Area in her own inimitable voice, which is California like no one else. She lays it out for you. With this writer, there is no halfsteppin'." —Susan Straight, author of Between Heaven and Here ☞ "Intense, riveting, spellbinding, this tour de force places the reader on the frontlines of the 1960's counter culture and the Black Power movement, one of the most turbulent times in American history. More than a coming of age novel, Virgin Soul is ultimately a meditation on love. It's about the love of Geniece's biological family and the family of radicals who adopt her. A must read."—Robert Alexander, author of "Servant of the People" ☞ "Judy Juanita gives readers a very real look at that exciting and turbulent time through the eyes of her strong, questing protagonist. There are pages when the prose lifts into lyricism, so it should be no surprise that the author's writing has for years encompassed poetry as well as reporting. This is her first novel. I'm glad she wrote it and hope it won't be her last." —P.J. Grath, book-seller, Dog Ears Books

Judy Juanita, née Judith Anne Hart in Berkeley, California, enrolled at 16 years old at Oakland City College where she met Huey Newton, Bobby Seale, and other radical students. Transferring to San Francisco State, she joined students in creating the country's first Black Student Union, first black studies program and open enrollment. She met up with Huey and Bobby again and began working full-time for the Black Panther Party. When  Eldridge Cleaver was jailed after the 1968 shootout, Huey appointed her editor-in-chief of the BPP newspaper. She worked on the newspaper and the Breakfast for Children program while finishing her B.A. At 23, she began teaching black journalism in SF State's historic black studies program.

In her debut novel, Virgin Soul, set in San Francisco-Oakland (Viking 2013), protagonist Geniece Hightower grows from naïveté into an independent woman in the tumult of the sixties and in the Black Panther Party.

Judy Juanita's plays have been performed in the Bay Area, L.A., NYC, Minneapolis and Winston-Salem, and her poetry and fiction widely published. She resides in Oakland.

CPSIA information can be obtained
at www.ICGtesting.com
Printed in the USA
LVOW08s1530240317
528385LV00003B/344/P